L♥VE BITES

L♥VE BITES

101 tips for dating guys with fangs

CLAIRE HOOPER

ABC
Books

The ABC 'Wave' device is a trademark of the
Australian Broadcasting Corporation and is used
under licence by HarperCollins*Publishers* Australia.

First published in Australia in 2010
by HarperCollins*Publishers* Australia Pty Limited
ABN 36 009 913 517
harpercollins.com.au

HarperCollins*Publishers*
25 Ryde Road, Pymble, Sydney, NSW 2073, Australia
31 View Road, Glenfield, Auckland 0627, New Zealand
A 53, Sector 57, Noida, UP, India
77–85 Fulham Palace Road, London W6 8JB, United Kingdom
2 Bloor Street East, 20th floor, Toronto, Ontario M4W 1A8, Canada
10 East 53rd Street, New York NY 10022, USA

National Library of Australia Cataloguing-in-Publication data:

Hooper, Claire.
    Love bites : 101 tips for dating guys with fangs / Claire Hooper.
    ISBN: 978 0 7333 2883 1 (pbk.)
    Vampires.
    Dating (Social customs)
    Australian Broadcasting Corporation.
398.45

Cover and internal design by Jane Waterhouse, HarperCollins Design Studio
Cover images: Woman by Lisa Peardon/Getty Images;
    all other images by shutterstock.com
Author photograph by James Peulidis
Typeset in 10.5/15pt Nofret Light by Kirby Jones

I dedicate this book to my husband,
even though when I asked him to make me
a cup of tea in return, he refused.
Vampires are such difficult men.

AUTHOR'S NOTE

Human beings have feared vampires for about as long as we've been cooking with fire. In fact, we've written a lot about both: currently the two biggest sections in your local bookstore are cookery and vampires.

Ancient peoples from all over the world told tales of demons or spirits who drank blood or inhabited corpses, and in the last few centuries these stories have been set down in print for our terrified titillation: John Polidori's *The Vampyre*, Bram Stoker's *Dracula*, Anne Rice's *Vampire Chronicles*.

But when did we start to *love* them?

It was around the time a certain blonde vampire slayer started looking at her prey-thing as more of a plaything (*Buffy*, season one) that we were bitten. And by the time this latest wave of vampires hit us, the poison had done its work – whether in the 'sparkle in the sun' or the 'addicted to his blood' camp, we were completely and irreversibly converted. We were 'vampire inclined'.

The increased immortal traffic on our screens has enabled those of us with humble imaginations or busy schedules to skip reading entirely and turn on the TV for a hit of sexy fang. In the last decade or so it's become common for any hot male actor worth his salt to eventually end up playing a vampire on screen – Brad Pitt in *Interview with a Vampire*, David Boreanaz in *Angel*, Stephen Moyer in *True Blood*, Robert Pattinson in *Twilight*, to name just a few. What's more, we've stopped idolising the actor and we just want the vampire they're portraying. Ask any girl: Edward Cullen or Robert Pattinson? There's no question. Does Mr Pattinson sparkle in the sun? No. Does Mr Cullen let his eyebrows grow into a mono? No. The immortal wins over the mortal every time.

Mind you, do vampires *really* sparkle in the sun? Was Stephenie Meyer correct when she altered the vampire myth? We will discuss this later in the book. After all, you wouldn't want to find out the hard way, after you've gone to all the trouble of snaring yourself a gorgeous immortal. You can't get a cold, hard embrace from a handful of ashes …

So if a living, breathing star like Brad Pitt can't compare to our fanged fantasy man, then our poor mortal admirers don't stand a chance. No wonder teen girls are breaking it off with their boyfriends, and young marrieds are sleeping on the couch with their copy of *Breaking Dawn* (and young men everywhere are taking out their frustration by mercilessly teasing emos). We have decided. We can only love a vampire.

But that's easier said than done.

Even if we knew where to find one, how would we know how to win his heart while keeping ourselves safe, without a decent instructional guide? I mean, you can't just pick up *The Joy of Sex* and draw fangs in. (Well, you can. Who hasn't, in lonely moments when the Kmart men's underwear catalogue, with fangs drawn in, just wasn't enough?)

That's where this book comes in. It may be the most important book you'll ever read about dating a vampire. In fact it could be the *only* book you'll ever read about dating a vampire. Because, let's face it, there are not many women with the experience that qualifies them to give advice on this very unique subject.

Okay, so technically I haven't *actually* dated a vampire. But I have dated a goth and a carny,* so I'm an expert when it

---

* Short for 'carnival folk'. Includes fire-eaters, tent-riggers and anyone whose job it is to yell 'Three balls for a fiver'. (Note that this group does not include mime artists. Pulease, I do have some standards.) The popular belief about carnies is that they smell, are missing teeth and will steal anything that is not nailed down, including children (who really should never be nailed down). However, I'm pleased to report that my carny was polite, didn't steal anything from me and had every one of his teeth. I can completely confirm the odour, though. What is that smell? Rotting thermals and grass clippings? Optimism? A hot dog in a bum bag?

comes to guys who can't go out in sunlight, aren't suitable to introduce to your parents, and quite possibly have blood on their hands.

I've also tried to make it work with a struggling actor, a guy with substance-abuse problems, an American, someone way hotter than me (twice) and someone way out of my age group (many times), so you see there's no-one better than me to ask you the most important question in the whole book:

Are you sure you don't just want a nice guy from the suburbs who works in the city and wears T-shirts to bed and calls his mother on a Sunday?
Think about what you're getting yourself into: the uncertainty, the fear, never being able to get him on his mobile, the old-fashioned manners, the night-time visits, that cold, hard body, the superhuman strength, eyes that betray centuries of loneliness and a deep longing to drink deeply from you … oh boy, okay, you're right, ditch the nice guy and get reading.

But I warned you, all right?

Yes, vampires are hot right now. But that dolphin tattoo was hot once too, and how sorry are you now? That's on your ankle for the rest of your life. And you could end up regretting this even more. First you're just taking him to your work Christmas party because he already has his own suit, next he's convinced you to let him turn you and, bam!, 300 years later, he's long gone and you're left with some *really* permanent 'eternal life' issues. And you've still got that dolphin tattoo.

So before I start answering all your questions – how to meet a vampire, seduce a vampire, keep your flatmate safe from your vampire, hide the corpse and so on – I've got a few more questions for you, just to make sure it's really a vampire you want.

Did you just read a book about a vampire?

Yeah, I read that one too. But tell me, when you read that other book about the handsome sea captain, did you start hanging around the docks, looking for a man with salt-water rash on his inner thighs? Perhaps the best thing for you might be to read more books about single women who get validation from their jobs and their great circle of friends and who don't need dangerous men in their lives.

Have you been watching a TV show about vampires?

Again, I know what you're going through. Try this. Get some old episodes of *Buffy* instead, the ones that feature Spike. There's nothing like seeing that '90s peroxide hair on a man to give you the metaphorical cold shower you need to get over the whole vampire thing.

Are you naturally attracted to mysterious, dangerous, cold and unwell–looking men?

Think about whether you could get your fix from any of the following vampire-alternatives: a goth or a carny (as previously mentioned); an aspiring indie rocker with a drug problem; an ageing soap star about twenty years past his prime; anyone from Scotland. Promise me you'll try at least one of these first, just to get some vampire-simulating experience.

Are you fascinated by the supernatural?

Fair enough. Have you considered the romantic prospects of some of the safer and easier to come by supernaturals? Ghosts, werewolves, zombies, leprechauns … they all make enthusiastic lovers (I hear) and will freak your parents out just as much as a fanged one.

Another option is to find a practising human magician. You get all the basic extras of a vampire – amazing abilities, flamboyant clothing, pasty skin – with the added bonus that magicians are really grateful when women pay attention to them. Sure, they're not immortal, but after a few years with a magician, you'll be glad it's not going to last forever.

Do you actually wish you were a vampire: the walking dead, beautiful and cruel, sustaining yourself on the souls of innocent humans?

Get a job in TV.

Do you just long to have daylight hours without your boyfriend around?

Here's a tip. It's called 'a guy with a job'. It took me ages to catch on to this one too.

STILL SURE YOU WANT TO DATE A VAMPIRE?

Okay, let's get started.

BE PREPARED

♥

'Is a vampire going to be offended if I wear a crucifix? Just in case?'

No, he won't be offended, and he won't even have a problem touching it, unless it's made of silver. Silver will hurt him, the cross will not.

Religious artefacts were long believed to hold power against the undead but they are now known to have no effect. Not that the majority of vampires want this cleared up, obviously. It's very convenient to have people arming themselves with completely ineffectual weapons.

Vampires also find the holy water thing absolutely hilarious. Throw it on them and they'll laugh. In fact, they scornfully refer to human urine as 'holy water' – but they won't laugh if you throw that on them.

One old story that's definitely true, though, is that vampires can't enter your home without invitation. It's a bizarrely courteous rule that no vampire can break, and it's worth keeping in mind because this is the only way you can truly guarantee your safety against a vampire.

When you're going out to meet a vampire, feel free to wear some silver jewellery because he'll only respect your caution. He knows that you know that he and his kind are not to be trusted.

Also take a warm jacket, because if you do end up scoring a kiss, you don't want to be breaking it off because your teeth are chattering.

TIP 2
MIND GAMES

♥

'I've been told I'm really easy to read. Even normal people seem to know what I'm thinking at any time. What can I do to make myself more intriguing for the average telepathic vampire?'

Bless you. You're a sweet, open-minded innocent with no capacity for deceit.

Sweet person, meet vampire.

Even if you're cool, calm and collected by human standards, a vampire can smell your fear, read your intentions, and tell when you're pretending not to look at his pectorals. And he can hear snippets of thoughts (for example, 'Would you look at those pectorals!').

If you're planning on entering this dark underworld, you'll need to build up strong mental defences (even stronger than those freaking amazing pectorals). Not just to seem alluringly mysterious, but because it may save your life.

A simple exercise to keep a vampire out of your head is to practise thinking the same phrase over and over, so he'll hear nothing else. I've already given a suggestion of what *not* to think but some phrases I recommend are 'to be or not to be', 'left, left, left, right, left' or 'do the hokey pokey'.

If you prefer to keep it simple, just play circus music in your head.

You'll also want to practise keeping a straight face. Play some poker to see how it's done, and don't be afraid to use dark glasses – plenty of vampires do. And if you find you're hopeless at keeping a neutral expression, like I am, either just hit a strong facial expression – scorn, loathing, bra itch – and stick with it, or hit the Botox hard. Don't just jab the forehead area like the socialite ladies do, treat the entire face. He won't have time to read your thoughts when he's busy wondering why you only communicate in nostril flares.

Then when you really kick off the courtship (he still calls it that, so I can too) you may just have to let down your defences. You can't keep up all that hard work.

And if you want to play hard to get, you've got your work cut out for you. Because he can tell when your heart skips and he knows it's when he lifts an eyebrow. Your best chance is to try to *genuinely* convince yourself that he is bad news and you are not interested. To help you with that, keep reading for plenty of good reasons why he's a bad idea. I recommend you skip over the honeymoon section, though, because that stuff will only weaken your resolve.

HEART HEALTH

♥

'If he's, like, super fast and super strong, and I have no hope of competing with him anyway, well then there's no need for me to stay in shape, right? Cos I'm not really into exercise.'

That sounds fair, but you haven't taken into account the palpitations you get whenever he's near.

The painful pounding chest that accompanies an infatuation isn't usually life threatening, but this vampire's a lot dreamier than your previous loves. He's also designed to be fatally charming, so the fluttering heart will stick around a lot longer than the usual three weeks.

Add to that the vampire's extraordinary effect on blood. Whenever he leans towards you, your blood pumps faster and runs thinner in response to his closeness. You can almost feel your veins pulling towards the surface, as though desperate to give themselves to him.

So it's bad news for those of you who live a sedentary life – vampire love is *literally* hard on the heart.

I recommend preparing for a vampire relationship by doing regular cardio exercise, because nothing's duller than missing out on nights of passion while you're in hospital recuperating from a heart attack.

And while you're at it, you may as well throw in some squats and lunges, because on the off-chance that this leads to a permanent partnership, why not be sure you're committing to an eternity with glutes of steel?

HOME IS WHERE HIS UNBEATING HEART IS

♥

'There are no castles in my area. I guess that means there are no vampires in my area, right?'

Even back when people lived in castles, this wasn't true. Vampires live in all sorts of homes.

If a vampire can get his hands on a big, old dwelling such as a castle, an abandoned church or a stately manor home, then he's a happy bloodsucker. But while some vampires have the wealth to score themselves a palace, some have fallen on harder times or simply prefer the simple life, and live in the heart of a city or on the road.

Vampires' tastes in dwellings are quite contradictory. They like to have privacy, but they also like to be surrounded by large numbers of potential prey.

For the vegetarian vampire this is easy, as a home can be set up with other like-minded vampires out in the country, where the livestock is plentiful. These vampires are exactly the kind you'd like to meet, but sadly they don't often emerge to mix with humans. I, personally, have a theory about the Amish, but I should do some research before I go casting aspersions …

City vampires achieve a sense of privacy by living in densely populated areas, where the crime rates are so high that nobody looks at anyone else. They have a network of friends and a regular meeting place, and the fact that they have chosen an urban life most likely means they are interested in humans. While this is a good sign romantically, you can never forget that they might be 'interested' in the way you'd be 'interested in dessert'.

Some vampires are completely homeless. They live in storm drains, in the eaves of a warehouse and even under your house. Rather than keeping themselves clean and blending in with humans, homeless vampires rely on speed and stealth to stalk their prey. They are not great conversationalists, and are just one more good reason not to play in storm drains.

There is no doubt that the bigger the city, the more promising the vampire hunt will be, and not just if you can locate a vampire bar. For ideas on where else to go, read on.

WHERE'S MY VAMPIRE?

♥

'Where I live there are no cool bars, and I'm not really into the bar scene anyway. Am I going to be able to find myself a vampire to fall in love with?'

Well, unlike the best places to meet a man, you are not going to bump into your future immortal beloved at the supermarket, the gym or in the photocopy room at work. Which, if we're honest with ourselves, is part of what is so great about vampires – they don't hang out in supermarkets or gyms, and they don't do any photocopying.

The reality is that if you don't want to head to your local underground nightspot to find a vampire, the process is going to take you a lot longer. You need to find places he might visit, make yourself available and wait to be approached.

You can increase your chances of success by not wearing any perfume that will cover up your scent, and by making sure you've always got a good book. And the easiest place to start is the same place you'll find that good book – the library. Vampires read a lot, and human stories help them stay in touch with their own humanity. So it's the perfect place really, because you're guaranteed the sensitive, thoughtful type.

Vampires are also interested in music, particularly the music of their youth, so attend the opera and chamber music recitals. If you can't afford the tickets, wait outside in the foyer and try to look intriguing as the audience exits. Staring at the sky or writing in a journal are surefire ways to look intriguing.

You can also try finding places to sit after dark and contemplate passers-by where passers-by might not notice you, such as leafy corners of parks, the tops of tall stone walls and the dark edges of alleyways. Be aware, though, this method carries risks, because you're pretty vulnerable to attack from ill-intentioned vampires or, even worse, ill-intentioned humans.

It's worth gently pursuing the country vampire as well. Head to agricultural fairs after nightfall, and walk around alone. Keep an eye out for the country vamp. You'll know him because he's beautiful and he's the only one not chowing down on greasy fairground food. It's worth a try, because even if there's only a one per cent chance of taking home a vampire, there's a 100 per cent chance of taking home some quality homemade chutneys and a tray of coconut ice.

Pick-up Lines

♥

'He's been around for hundreds of years. Are there any pick-up lines he hasn't heard?'

When it comes to courtship between vampires and humans, the vampire is used to being the initiator, so he really hasn't heard many pick-up lines at all.

Therefore you can go for something pretty simple such as, 'Apart from being sexy, what are you doing for the rest of eternity?' or 'It's getting hot in here, can I use your body to cool down?' or 'I'd invite you over my threshold any day'.

Or if you're feeling really forward you could say, 'Let me get you a drink' and then sit down on a coaster.

Whatever you do, don't say, 'You're nearly as beautiful as I imagine Edward would be', and don't introduce yourself as Bella, even if that's your real name. Similarly, you shouldn't hop onto the barstool next to him and open with, 'So how many times have you read all four books? If it's less than five, I beat you'. And definitely do not ask him if he knows any wolves he can introduce you to.

You may be getting the idea that vampires aren't big *Twilight* fans, and they're not. Nothing turns them off as much as thinking you want them to be the lead character in your own teen romance novel. It's so ungrateful of them; they've never been so popular.

But popular they are, and so to ensure you stand out from the crowd, think about a more creative delivery. For example, you might want to deliver your pick-up line telepathically: 'Your legs must be tired. Cos you've been running through my mind all day.'

SHOW A BIT OF NECK

♥

'What's the deal with dressing to highlight your neck veins? Is it sexy? Or is it about as obvious as wearing a miniskirt short enough to show both your muffin top and muffin bottom?'

Classy turn of phrase; I'm sure glad it wasn't me who wrote that.

A vampire loves the way humans walk around all day showing their necks innocently to the world, without realising how much of a turn-on it is. To catch his eye, try a boat-neck top – that's a wide, high scoop – which makes the throat look mad sexy without looking like you're trying, and if you can make it seem casual, a side up-do for your hair.

To take it up a notch, for a third date or special occasion, a tight corset makes the pulse beat stronger in the neck. Find a delicate earring just long enough to tap lightly against your carotid artery every time you turn your head, and he will find it maddeningly distracting.

The carotid artery is the good one. It's pretty much pumping straight out of the heart. The jugular vein is right next to it, and it's the one pirates talk about slicing, although what they don't know is that they're really hitting the carotid at the same time, and that's what kills people faster. Pirates don't know much about anatomy. Nor do I, but I think I got that right.

A final note: don't get rid of all of your turtlenecks. If all goes well, you may end up needing a little more coverage at your office job.

TIP 8
DARK COLOURS

♥

'I'm a jeans and T-shirt girl. Should I dress more like a vampire to catch his eye?'

That depends. Are you talking capes? Cos if you're talking capes, the answer is no. Vampires don't wear capes anymore. In fact, none ever really did. Find me historical evidence of a vampire who wore a cape, other than The Count from *Sesame Street*, and I'll point out that it was technically a robe. Superheroes wear capes. And not the cool ones. Magicians wear capes. I rest my case.

Jeans and T-shirt are fine, especially if you're lucky enough to meet him somewhere other than a vampire bar.

If you do have to go looking and find yourself in a rat-infested alleyway at midnight in the dodgy part of town climbing down some stairs into a converted cellar, jeans and T-shirt are still fine, in fact you'll be glad you didn't go to much effort. But do consider picking a black T-shirt rather than a pastel one. A pink T-shirt with the words 'Drama Queen' on it is going to make you look like a tourist, and for heaven's sake don't wear any *Twilight* merchandise.

If you are already a little bit gothic when it comes to style, great. It's a sexy look. Just don't sacrifice comfort. Wear things you could still climb a tree in or shimmy down a drainpipe in, because you never know where the night will lead when you're hanging out with a vampire.

Try to stick with dark colours. Vampire life is all about blending into the shadows, and you don't want him worrying about your safety when your silver glitter stilettos are catching the moonlight.

TIP 9
GOTH COMEBACK

❤

'You just mentioned goths again. Earlier you said you'd dated one. Surely you're not old enough! Didn't they die out over ten years ago?'

Firstly, thank you, and secondly, you're right. I was lucky enough to date one of the very last goths, a really nice boy who was clever enough to try and goth it up in the sweltering heat of Perth, Western Australia.

And yes, I am old enough, okay? You'll have to get used to old people if you want to date vampires. They'll always be hitting you with baffling references like 'Don't go all Madame Bovary on me', 'That hep new Beethoven sound' and 'You're the Rachel to my Ross'. They are really old.

Goths are actually making a bit of a comeback, since the emos took the whole 'wearing black clothes and make-up and sitting in train stations' thing off the goths and then stuffed it up by listening to top 40 music and not having enough legitimate reasons to be sad. I'm predicting a big goth boom, much bigger than the goth scene of the '80s, if only because the current obesity boom will mean really big goths.

Sometimes you might have trouble discerning a vampire from a goth, especially in a poorly lit bar. Here's a tip: a vampire can't feel it if you kick him in the shin. A goth can feel it. He feels it in his shin and he feels it deep down where he keeps his feelings. Cos he really feels things. Boo hoo. Too cruel?

TIP 10
LOSE THE TAN

♥

'I'm the beachy type. Will my natural, healthy glow put him off?'

Pasty white skin is the best look you can go for to score yourself a vampire. It visually says, 'Not only am I ready to spend the rest of my life out of the sunlight, but I already do.'

A tan can make a vampire doubt whether you are the girl for him. Not only because he would feel guilty that dating him would make you sleep in and miss out on surfing the best breaks of the day (or whatever it is you beachy girls do) but because it's the one physical attribute he can never attain.

It's like trying to pick up a bald guy by going on and on about how much you love having your hair washed.

And even if you think you look sexier with a tan, don't even consider using that spray-on stuff. Fake tan, to a vampire, looks about as classy as doing blackface on TV.

TIP 11
THE SUNLIGHT ISSUE

♥

'While we're talking tans, isn't it about time you addressed the question of light sensitivity? After all, we are at Tip 11 already.'

The quick answer is 'Yes, vampires are sensitive to sunlight'.*

A quality of the vampire 'curse' is that they are suspended in a version of their physical state at the moment they became a vampire. This is almost always at night or in darkness, and results in melanin-free skin and dilated pupils, which means that they can see clear detail at night and appear to 'glow', but also that sunlight is piercingly painful for their eyes and, yes, does burn their skin.

Not powerfully enough to make them explode if caught in a sunbeam, mind you. That only happens in movies, along with people hacking security systems in 15 seconds and prostitutes who look like Julia Roberts.

It is believed that humans can be 'turned' at dusk. The resulting vampires will have less aversion to sunlight and so can walk among us, but have far inferior night hunting

---

* A quicker answer would be 'Yes' but then you'd have to say, 'Yes, what?' and I'd say, 'The thing you asked' and you'd say, 'Right, you mean yes, vampires are sensitive to sunlight' and it would all take way longer.

abilities, so will likely need to feed in daylight. This might explain tabloid journalists.

Your average vampire has many tricks at his disposal for short stints in the daylight, from just sunglasses and a long-sleeved shirt, to old magic enchantments, but the easiest way, of course, is for him to stick to the shadows.

Ask your vampire what his level of light sensitivity is and be respectful when he prefers his beach dates by moonlight.

For god's sake, don't pull him outside into the sun at midday 'just to see what it looks like'. It will be as much of a warning sign for him as if you asked him 'if he knew anyone called Edward'.

TIP 12
VIRGIN BLOOD

💙

'I know vampires are really into virgins. Can I just tell him I am one? He's not going to bother asking around to find out the truth is he?'

Vampires are into virgins, sure, but they're into non-virgins as well. Basically, they're into anything that's full of human blood, so this covers pretty much all humans.

The myth about the virgin's appeal grew out of Victorian-era attitudes to women's sexuality, which still linger today. You know, like 'no frotting out of wedlock', 'only floozies show their knees' and 'a girl who'd flash her breasts on YouTube is not marriage material'. That sort of old-fashioned nonsense.

Anyway, if the relationship does end up getting physical then your virgin status is not going to be as exciting to him as whether or not you've been bitten before. He would kind of like to know he's the first to have had that pleasure.

If your instinct is to fib about how many sexual partners you've had, reconsider. Even if his mind-reading ability is not perfect, he will have mastered the basic skill of being able to smell when someone is lying to him.

For proof that vamps are not exclusively looking for virgins, observe that they hang out in forests and late-night bars, not internet-gaming cafés and Dick Smith electronics stores.

HEIGHT DIFFERENCE

♥

'I'm falling for a vampire who's about three inches shorter than me. Is there any point in pursuing this relationship? Surely he'd feel threatened by a taller girlfriend?'

Really? Threatened?

It's possible you may have skipped some of the earlier information – the stuff about vampires being impossibly strong and fast and not having the slightest fear of humans … remember that?

To be physically threatening to a vampire, you would have to be over ten feet tall with two giant wooden stakes for legs. Maybe you are, in which case try prosthetics, for his sake, because compromise is part of a healthy relationship.

When it comes to making a romantic connection, a vampire is first attracted to your smell and your vulnerability, and if he shows interest beyond that it's because he's fascinated by unique things about you* – your mannerisms, your turn of phrase, your ideas and (although he won't admit it) your potential for eternal life. He is also much

---

* Although sometimes you'll find out it's just because you remind him of an ex-girlfriend. Yeah, vampires do that too.

less affected by your 'calendar modelling potential' than a regular mortal man.

You will find that one of the vampire's many attractive qualities is his complete lack of concern at your physical shortcomings (or tallcomings). Excessive height, strength or sporting prowess, or the lack of: none of these bother him.

A vampire won't even be threatened by phenomenal good looks because they themselves are a phenomenon so unnervingly stunning that people need a little lie down if they look for too long.

So don't worry about your height.

No need to wear stilettos though. Not because they make you taller than him, but because they look a bit like stakes.

DROP DEAD

♥

'Apparently all vampires are drop-dead gorgeous. Well, I'm not drop-dead gorgeous and I'm wondering if there are any plainer vampires who might be interested in dating me?'

It's interesting you should use the phrase 'drop-dead gorgeous' because, essentially, that's the purpose of the vampire's good looks. They look much as they did when they were alive, but with a little extra magic thrown in to make it easier for them to seduce their prey.

However, there is a range of attractiveness in the vampire world. Plenty of them started out as less attractive humans, and since the vampire world works on the same popularity model as a human high school, chances are these guys are more likely to be single and not tied up servicing the needs of some vampire queen. And they will still make your knees weaker than any human you've ever met.

Your choice of the phrase 'drop-dead gorgeous' is also interesting because it suggests you may be an older reader. Have you ever referred to vampires as being 'spunky' or 'natty dressers'? If you were born before 1965, then you may be worried that you are going to look a bit older than the average vampire.

There are some silver foxes out there for you – men who were in the late of their prime when they became immortal. Not many, though, I'll warn you, because the older a man gets, the less likely it is that his heart will be able to take the stress of a transition. And you will need determination to fight off the advances of all the older female vampires. They may be older but they're still pretty hot and know how to get what they want. They're like the female cast of *Friends* from the last season. Actually, there are some rumours about those girls …

GAY VAMPIRE LOVE

♥

'I started reading this book under the mistaken impression that it would cater to gay, male readers as well. One quick question before I go ask for a refund: is there a vampire gay scene, and are there any differences to the dating rules?'

Thank you for your question, and for the disappointed tone. You may be interested to know that a gay version of this book is soon to be released. If you can't wait until it comes out,* my tip is to go through the book with a white corrector pen and change all the pronouns from 'she' to 'he', and then draw a moustache on the cover, which is pretty much all I'll be doing.

In answer to your question, there is not really a gay scene. The vampire population is simply not large enough to support individual 'scenes', although 'families' of a certain preference may group together.

You'll also find that in the vampire world, the lines between straight and gay are blurred. Vampires are lustful creatures, but regular sexual lust is all mixed up with blood lust, which makes sexual orientation less important. Plus, the

---

* Gay joke.

lack of choice arising from such a small vampire dating pool means they are not so picky about gender.

There are no special vampire gay clubs, but then, given the borderline flamboyant style of clothing favoured by most vamps, how would you even know if you'd walked into a vampire gay club?

It is, however, possible to learn to recognise the more committed gay vampire from his clothing. For example, he will not be wearing a cape (see Tip 8), but he *may* be wearing a capelet. A capelet is shorter than a cape, but if you're not sure, try calling it a cape and wait to see if he corrects you.

The gay vampire might have a little umbrella in the glass of blood he is drinking and he could even be engaged in one of his favourite hobbies – using his unique powers of seduction on a homophobic redneck man at the bar. This is an act of retribution for the cruelty he experienced during his human adolescence. He likes to leave a souvenir bite mark somewhere on them to remind them of him whenever they take a shower.

CHANGING YOUR MIND

♥

'I've met a vampire and I can't stop thinking about her. That's right, I said "her". Can vampires turn you gay?'

One of the most well-known of the vampire's deadly tricks is the ability to charm their prey. If they didn't, their victim's blood would become sticky with fear and adrenaline, so they seduce you to get a smooth beverage. If they want to, they can be pretty close to irresistible.

In the case of the guy from Tip 15 (if he hasn't returned this book for a refund yet), this means he could be surprised to find himself desperately in love with a vampire of the *opposite* sex, if she decided to make it so.

So if you're in love with someone who's not your usual type, that means she probably turned it on for you. She wanted to kill you and changed her mind, or wanted to make you love her. Either way, consider yourself lucky. (But carry a stake in case she's just saving you as a snack for later.)

You are reading this book because you want to be dating a vampire. And once you've started daydreaming about a gentleman caller who is *no longer alive* and *older than your grandfather* surely it's not much more of a hurdle that your gentleman caller is not a gentleman?

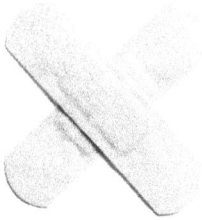

BOYFRIEND UPGRADE

♥

'I've already got a boyfriend. Can I get him changed into a vampire?'

What a lucky guy your boyfriend is.

I suppose you think you're being respectful to him by asking that question instead of just dumping him, but then you'd have to go to all the trouble of finding yourself a new vampire beau.

Has it ever occurred to you that this request might be slightly more of a big deal than him suggesting, say, that you lose a few pounds, or use slightly less perfume, or say 'please' more often when you send him to the shops for a Cherry Ripe (which, by the way, he wouldn't dare to request of you)?

And let's face it, if he had the guts, he'd probably love to ask *you* to change into a vampire, to save him the trouble of finding himself someone better.

Why not do something for him, for a change? Hunt down a vampire who'll agree to make you immortal and reveal yourself as a Valentine's surprise for your boyfriend. You'll be super sexy, super powerful, eternally young and, to be honest, you couldn't be more of a parasite than you already are.

TIP 18
BEDTIME

♥

'I've heard vampires don't sleep, but if that's true, what do they need the coffins for?'

Back in the old days, when a person was turned into a vampire, they would be found 'dead' and their family would have them put into a coffin. A few days later they would wake, ready to leave the coffin and, if they were lucky, they wouldn't have been buried yet. While vampires can claw their way out of six feet of soil, the effort is going to leave them starving for blood with only a few minutes before dawn, and no clean clothes to hunt in.

The coffin is a big part of their mythology. For older vampires, there's a sentimental attachment; for younger vampires, it's just a cool decorating item.

Vampires are severely weakened by the sun, so they will find a dark place to wait out the daylight hours, and a coffin is as good a place as any. They will also need to rest if they have been hurt in battle, if they are hungry, or if they are very, very old.

But get this: many 'sleep' with their eyes open. It will have begun as a tactic to keep safe from slayer attacks, but now it's just a habit, and it looks pretty creepy.

So if you're thinking about taking a romantic afternoon nap with one of these 'starey sleepers', either he needs to wear an eye mask, or you do.

Or just accept that he's happy enough in your company to lie there and watch you sleep. Sorry, is that as creepy as sleeping with your eyes open? Well, I've got news for you: if he thinks anything of you at all he's already watched you during plenty of private moments. Think of that next time you have a sneaky nose pick.

THE LITTLE ROOM

♥

'If, like you say, he's watching me when I sleep, does that also mean he's watching me when I pee? And worse? Isn't that going to gross him out?'

I've got bad news for you: it's no grosser for him than watching you eat.

The good news is that neither grosses him out much. Along with napping and shaving (yes, he watches that too), eating and abluting are just a few of the things he vaguely remembers from his old human life and, over time, they've begun to seem boring and a little alien to him.

Even better news: he can't see through walls. So since most toilets don't have viewing windows, he can only sense what you're doing and thinking, and unless you start talking to yourself about what's happening ('Wow, that's bigger than usual for a weekday' etc.) you will have a modicum of privacy.

So going to the toilet definitely won't gross him out. At worst he will feel a little nostalgic for the days when he'd sit down for a session with the Sunday paper. Pee freely, and remember, holding it in will only have far grosser consequences.

TIP 20
HEAD COLDS

♥

'I've got a really bad cough and a runny nose. Do we need to stay apart for a few days so he doesn't catch it?'

Your cold has about as much chance of hurting him as hitting him on the head with a shovel would.

(He can barely feel that, by the way. If you don't believe me, ask him and I guarantee he'll let you hit him on the head with a shovel. Flat side, not blade-first – obviously, that might make a dent. Do it in private, too, not right in the middle of the hardware store.)

Even if you were planning a bit of a bitey make-out session, the cold wouldn't be a problem for him. Sure you'll smell a little different, but in the first few days of your cold, you're blood will be surging with the white blood cells of your immune system response, which is the vampire equivalent of a pizza with extra cheese – pretty tasty.

If you were sick with something that could hurt him, he would still need to drink your blood to become contaminated, so just keep your snuggling light.

And if you just feel too gross to see him and are looking for an excuse, tell him you have come down with a touch of one of the following non-vampire-friendly sicknesses: malaria; Ross River virus; 24-hour hepatitis; or reverse-haemophilia.

Although he may correctly guess that the last ones are made up.

DANCING

♥

'Does dating a vampire mean giving up going out dancing?'

Vampires are great dancers, regardless of how much of a klutz they were as mortals. Their supernatural grace and precision make a spin around the floor a breeze.

Note that I say 'spin around the floor', though. Your vampire beau needs the right kind of music to look sexy.

It's like the phenomenon you observe when you catch your parents dancing to the music of their youth, and miraculously all that wooden arm swinging and foot shuffling becomes poetry in motion.

So, drop the needle on anything olde worlde (or if it must be chart music, anything ballady) and magic will happen. His waltz is divine, and he may even manage a jive or a graceful solo turn on an '80s dance floor, if only by virtue of the fact that his look is already borderline 'New Romantic'.

But take him to a hip-hop club and suddenly that perfect posture and tucked in shirt will look certifiably 'undead'.

Musical styles that require a wide range of uninhibited movement – electro-pop, metal, urban crossover, alt-country, dance-floor anthems – are just not for your guy. That's werewolf music.

For example, he might enjoy listening to Lady Gaga but let him try dancing to it and it may be the worst day of your life. You may even stop loving him. Nobody wants that.

And there's some music he won't even enjoy *listening* to. Little known fact: R & B is like nails on a chalkboard for vampires (and some others of us), so if you're ever caught without your perfectly sharpened stake, you can also ward off unfriendly vampires by turning on your stereo and cranking the Boyz II Men.

TIP 22

BAKE SALE

♥

'Why is his cooking so much better than mine? He doesn't even eat! It's insulting to me as a woman!'

Frankly, I find your implication that cooking is for women insulting to me as a woman. I'll have you know I haven't met a man yet who didn't cook better than me. But enough about my lack of domestic skills …

Your sweetheart has spent several centuries waiting for you to come along, and once he read all of Dickens, skimmed the entire Shakespeare catalogue, giggled his way through Bram Stoker's *Dracula*, didn't quite finish *War and Peace*, and then learnt Russian so he could not quite finish *War and Peace* again, he still had several decades before TV was invented in which to get desperate enough to read cookbooks. That's why most of his best dishes are from the depression through to World War II – syrup cake, poor man's pudding, slow-roasted pigeon, that sort of thing.

He's great at it because, although he doesn't eat, he has a phenomenal sense of smell. He doesn't need to sample it as he goes along, because he can identify every ingredient just from their aroma. He couldn't actually sample it even if he wanted to. As strong as his sense of smell is, his sense of taste is weak, and if he swallows food he then has to throw it up, lest it sit in his insides and rot. Given his strong sense of smell, this is pretty unpleasant for him. Not great for you either.

The mention of unpleasant smells brings us to the big question. Can he cook with garlic?

Garlic is a pungent smell that masks other smells. The vampire doesn't like it. If you eat it, it will affect the smell of your blood, which makes it an effective mosquito repellent and, to a point, a vampire repellent … if maybe you were dealing with a well-fed vampire, while standing in a group of delicious, blood-filled people who hadn't eaten any garlic at all. Not so much if you were alone in a forest standing face to face with a ravenous, recently turned vampire. A couple of slices of bruschetta earlier in the evening is just not going to cut it then.

So he could probably cook with garlic, but he's not likely to. Smelling it on you is bad enough, but the way that odour lingers on his fingers is just so annoying.

TIP 23
LOVE BITES

♥

'Can he accidentally "turn" me? I mean, say we got a bit carried away and I let him bite me and now I'm feeling a bit flushed and light-headed … Could it be happening to me?'

Firstly, he can't accidentally turn you. He can accidentally kill you, but it's a big job to take you to the brink of death, stop the second before it's too late and then make you drink from his blood before your heart stops beating. It's not something you can do without meaning to.

It would be about as easy as converting a car to electric power or completing a tax return or changing a quilt cover without meaning to.

It would be about as easy as *accidentally* converting a car to electric power or *accidentally* completing a tax return or *accidentally* changing a quilt cover.

So you're okay.

The big question is now you know you're in the clear, does it feel like the time you sighed with relief over a pregnancy test and then experienced an inexplicable sense of loss?

Did you want it to happen?

If the idea of becoming one of his kind is on your mind, it's time to have a talk about what you would like him to do if something happened and he had to choose between letting you die and giving you eternal life.

Whatever your preference, just be honest with him because even though he says he can't read your mind, he actually kind of can.

TIP 24
SILVER

♥

'All of my jewellery is silver, which I've heard can hurt vampires. Is this why I'm not getting any vampire phone numbers, and is there something I can coat the silver with so I'm less repellent?'

First of all, let's address other possible reasons that a vampire may find you repellent. Are you, for example, heading out wearing fake vamp teeth? Do you have a three-bulb-a-day garlic addiction? Does your silver jewellery spell out the words 'fangbanger69'?

If it is your jewellery scaring them off, then the simple answer is don't wear the jewellery.

Wearing too much silver jewellery around vampires is like turning up to speed dating wearing a vest covered with cans of Mace. It looks a little over-cautious. Possibly even aggressive …

Draping yourself in abundant decorations is fine, but you're going to have to go up-market (pricey platinum) or down-market (silver-painted plastic). The good news is most people can't tell the difference, so I'd recommend down-market.

But you should put your silver away in the jewellery box for now.

Coating the jewellery will not reduce its harmful properties. What were you going to use, anyway? Nail polish? Fly spray? WD-40?

Silver is a pure metal and is one of the few substances with some power over the vampire, who can be warded off or tied up with silver jewellery. The vampire will still recognise the danger of silver from beneath any coating you apply.

Here's the really interesting bit. The undead are very superstitious, and their superstitions dictate which objects have power over them. Hence, the toxicity of silver, and also the old 'invited over the threshold' principle (as mentioned in Tip 1) and the idea of not being able to walk on consecrated ground or cross running water.

Which is why religious iconography such as crosses and holy water are no longer found in the slayer's arsenal – they only held power when both vampire and human possessed unwavering faith.

This is also a warning about the power of the vampire and how you can never be quite sure what will keep you safe around one with bad intentions.

The stronger he is, of mind and body, the less power your human weapons will have over him.

Oh, but beheading works. That *definitely* works.

So, when you do make a date, you'd better be pretty sure you've taken his heart. Or you're going to need to take his head …

TIP 25

PLAYING THE FIELD

♥

'Are all vampires looking to mate for life, or are some interested in dating multiple partners? More importantly, am I allowed to date multiple vampires?'

There are so many kinds of vampire relationships. The 'mate for life' type is a minority, despite what some of the more recent literature would suggest (I'm talking *Twilight*). Their community accepts the concept of marriage, but most consider eternity to be a very long time and will either make short-term commitments, or no commitment at all.

Let me assure you that you're best off looking for the 'marriage' guy, even if you're not really into marriage. When it comes to boyfriends without souls, it helps to find one with remnants of old-fashioned morality. Because he's also likely to have traces of other human courtesies, such as holding human life sacred and knowing it's not polite to read your emails. (Though he can probably read them telepathically, anyway. Vampires' amazing mental powers have evolved alongside technology.) And, seriously, marriage isn't so bad. You're mortal, after all, so it's not like it's forever.

If you do get into the swinging scene, be careful. A powerful vampire is likely to cultivate a harem as a demonstration of status. You can join one of these harems, but given a human is considered more a commodity than a lover, he will definitely not want to share you with others, and if you displease him you will be readily disposed of. The method of disposal will make you nostalgic for the guy who dumped you by text.

PATIENCE

♥

'I've met this beautiful boy who's always on my train home at night. Well, I say "met", but all we've done is look at each other. The other night when we were the only people in the carriage, he smiled and lifted his lip just enough to show me his sharply defined teeth. I looked away and when I looked back he was gone. I haven't seen him since. I am pretty sure he's the real thing, but will I ever see him again?'

It's clear he's noticed you, and it will have been a big thing for him to reveal himself to you like that. He may be unsure whether he's done the right thing.

The problem is that any vampire with a conscience will not want to ruin your life by getting romantically involved. You can only hope that he finds you fascinating enough that his curiosity outweighs his caution.

In the meantime, there's little you can do. He knows where to find you, if he wants to, and when it feels right, he will. So there's no point riding the train endlessly, waiting and hoping.

The one thing you can try is a note. Leave it on the train or drop it as you walk home. It's a long shot, but if he is watching from a distance, he might pick it up. Say something like, 'I like you, come back.' That's sweet. Nothing too full on, like: 'You are, aren't you? Oh. My. God. Can you bite me just a little?'

But, like I said, you really can't hurry him.

This situation is difficult for you, because time passes differently for mortals and immortals. He is used to spending months, or even years, waiting. You need to decide whether you can wait that long. Just think, you might miss out on some great dates. And, frankly, a girl who has spent six months pining for someone she's never spoken to can start to look a little gloomy and desperate. In fact, he might not even recognise you when he reappears.

Oh, and it's worth mentioning that he might not have been a vampire at all. He might have just had a weird smile.

Is he a vampire?

♥

'I'm falling in love with this guy who claims to be one ... like, he's pale and cold and beautiful but, here's the thing, he can't read my mind. I know because I telepathically asked him to bite me, and he didn't. But he did ask me to lend him twenty bucks. Have I mistakenly picked up a junkie?'

It's hard to know for sure and, in the early stages of the relationship, there are a lot of similarities. For example, he will become gradually tenser around you until he needs to disappear for a few hours. His pupils will frequently change size and, like a vampire, you may find him sleeping with his eyes open. Although, if you do find your guy like this you should call an ambulance, because in his case it's not called 'sleep', it's called 'an overdose'.

Take care, and if you have fallen for a junkie, you can probably count yourself lucky. He may have an inconvenient addiction but, as a boyfriend, he's going to be a lot less trouble than a vampire. Think about it. At least you can get him on his mobile (well, when he's paid his bill). And his friends don't want to eat you, which is always a bonus.

Not only that, but at least you won't be the one with puncture marks.

SUPERPOWERS

♥

'Well, I'd just like to express my sympathies for that last girl, who has clearly been duped by a junkie. I, however, have found myself a vampire who can't read my mind, but as yet has not asked to borrow twenty dollars. Explain that, if you can.'

I really should have stressed this in the last tip, but an apparent lack of mind-reading abilities doesn't necessarily mean he isn't a vampire.

In some cases, the human can be harder than usual to read. Or perhaps he's just choosing to ignore what's on your mind. Or maybe he was just a particularly imperceptive man in his former life. In which case, he may need more time and practice to build up his mind-reading abilities.

He probably has other magnificent skills, though; things he was very good at as a human, which are further amplified now.

For example, he may be able to tell you whether it will rain tomorrow or the name of a song after hearing just the first bar. And, if you're really lucky, he may even have some skills that you can't find on the average iPhone.

For example, some vampires are blessed with unusual strength, charm or even healing powers, because that's what they brought from their old life.

If I were a vampire, I know I'd be awesome at making lists and telling people what to do. What can I say? It's a gift.

HISTORY LESSONS

♥

'I know he's really, really old, so, like, how much do I have to know about history? We're both hot. Isn't that enough to have in common? Cos I'm not really interested in history.'

Listen, love, if you're interested in him, you're interested in history.

If you're not interested in history, then you're just interested in the way he looks, and how good he'd look standing next to you. But you're never going to see how good you look together, not in the mirror, not on your camera phone. So are you sure you can be bothered?

It doesn't sound like you're looking for a very deep relationship anyway, so perhaps the best course of action is for you to find your way to an underground vampire bar and hunt down a bloodsucker who is looking to extend his harem of really hot women. He'll happily welcome another girl who doesn't care about his past.

Mind you, you also sound like you don't really like hard work, and it takes a lot of investigation and persistence to locate a vampire bar, so, again, are you sure you can be bothered?

Maybe you should go back to dating sports stars, and give the vampires back to the girls who really appreciate them: bookish archeology students in their op-shop dresses; bedroom electronic musicians who never go out in the sunlight; shy night-shift nurses hoping for an encounter with a vampire; and book-writing comedians who always walk down alleyways instead of the main street, just in case, even though cobblestones are murder in heels …

Because *they* are all interested in history, especially when it's so good-looking.

AGE LINES

♥

'Hey, when was the Black Plague? Because he claims he's only been a vampire for 105 years. But somehow the plague came up in conversation and he acted really touchy when I said something about it probably being all the dirty people who died. I think he might have been there. How old does that make him, and why would he lie?'

It does sound like he might have been there, and may have lost someone dear to him. It is also possible that he was saved from dying in the plague by a vampire who took a shine to him and created what you now see. This could be a traumatic memory, and you shouldn't push him to talk about it.

That said, it's pretty dodgy to go around lying about your age.

Especially when being alive during the Black Plague would make his actual vampire age over 750 years. Or, to put it another way, well over six centuries older than he's claiming. Or, to put it yet another way, really freaking old.

Now, he could be the age he says he is, and he's touchy because he once loved a vampire who was old enough to have lost someone in the Black Plague.

But if he is fibbing, it might be because he's trying to get you to fall for him and doesn't want to scare you away with a really big number. (It's funny that it hasn't occurred to him that 105 is also a really big number.) And, despite what people say about lying being bad, it can be a really good sign that he's into you and wants to make it easy for you to like him.

Hopefully, he's not lying about his age because he's really obsessed with youth. It'd be hard, as a mortal, to maintain a relationship with someone this hung up on age. Nobody wants to be issued an ultimatum like, 'So you either lose your soul, or we get you a little Botox. You're twenty-two now and it's really starting to show …'

BIRTH CERTIFICATE

💜

'You didn't really answer my question in the last tip. How do I know how old he is then?'

If you really want to know whether he's a fresh-faced baby of eighty-three, or an experienced 762, you can't just sneak a look at his birth certificate. If there's one thing vampires are good at, it's forging official documents.

Instead, keep your ears out for a couple of telling phrases. For example, if he ever accidentally lets slip that he owned a slave, this makes him 150 years old, minimum. Two hundred and fifty if he's got a British accent.

If he ever mentions having worn a ruff, this places him at 400 or over. A ruff was an item of clothing that fell out of fashion in the early 1600s, and you do not want to see a picture of him wearing one, trust me. Ruffs look not dissimilar to the buckets that dogs wear on their heads when they have stitches, except that they're made out of doilies.

The final clue is if you ever hear a Dad Joke. In mortal men, the transistion from actual humour to Dad Jokes happens around the age of thirty-five to fifty, and for vampires (because they're a bit classier) at around 500 years. Consider him older than that if he ever says 'Pull my finger', 'Hi Hungry, I'm Thomas', or 'This cemetery is popular. People are dying to get in'.

FRENCH KISSING

♥

'Excuse my innocence, but is it really possible to kiss a vampire safely? I mean, aren't their teeth sharp enough to draw blood if they so much as brush against your lips?'

I understand your concern, but kissing a vampire is no more difficult than kissing with braces. Plus it's infinitely more enjoyable.

Think about it. Vampires' teeth may be sharper than other guys', but they're not so much longer that they get in the way. And how often during a passionate kiss do you get lips on teeth action? Not very often. Teeth on teeth, sure, that happens all the time, and to the best of us, but you should be able to kiss without munching on each other's mouths.

What I'm saying is you can't get bitten by accident, so you don't need to feel scared.

If he's a nice vampire, he'll go especially gentle on you the first time. And he'll understand if you're keeping it pretty conservative.

If he's a nasty vampire, frankly it's too late to be worrying about him nipping your lips, because he's probably got some big plans for your neck, and they're not particularly romantic.

GSOH

♥

'Vampires in the movies always look so serious. But I'm a comedy fan. Do vampires have a sense of humour?'

Sure they do! They like clever word play or a good double act and they'll get a great belly laugh from watching you get over-excited and hurt yourself. (The human equivalent is how we enjoy laughing at our dogs when they spazz out and run into glass sliding doors. Oh, not funny? Just me? Well, me and vampires. They would laugh at a dog running into a pane of glass too. Totally.)

I'm generalising though; vampires' tastes in comedy are pretty much as diverse as humans', and are informed by their tastes before they became immortal.

The only form of comedy they will all struggle to enjoy is the sitcom, for example, *Two and a Half Men.* They may have all of eternity, but they don't have time for that half-hour of human debris.

TELEVISION

♥

'Hi, me again, from the question before … So does that mean that when it comes to TV, they'd rather watch drama, or that they don't really like TV at all?'

No, they love TV. In fact, there are plenty of vampires working in TV. Think about it – they never age, they're super powerful, they can amass legions of followers – Oprah, anyone? I'm not saying categorically that America's talk-show sweetheart is Queen of the Vampires; I'm just saying it's possible.

There is a rumour that a vampire was the inventor of an early form of television. It makes sense, because the vampire community had been surviving on books and radio for a really long time, so would have been keen to find new ways to avoid going outside. More recently, vampires have been thrilled with the invention of portable gaming devices and Sudoku. Entertaining yourself for an eternity really is a chore.

So grab yourself the *Buffy* box set and settle in for a marathon together this weekend … Oh, I forgot to mention that in the last tip – he absolutely pisses himself at *Buffy*. All immortals find Buffy funny. Must be something to do with how unrealistically easily she kills vampires …

TIP 35
LOSE THE ADMIRERS

♥

'My vampire's a private sort of guy, so I'm the only one who knows the reason why he's so supernaturally beautiful, but I'm not the only one who's noticed that he is. He is constantly stared at by other women. What can I do to discourage it?'

Not much. And you can't be too mad at these girls. They're only noticing what you noticed in the first place. But you might find that if you are seen out and about more often as a couple, there will be less focus on him. If only because his admirers will now be watching you instead, and wondering what it is you've got that they haven't.

Hopefully they will watch hard enough to notice how attentive he is to you and how sweet you are together, and perhaps then they'll finally back off. This method does have its downsides, though. While going into hiding and only appearing on rare occasions can make him more intriguing, being seen out more often might just make him seem attainable to all those female fans.

So, unfortunately, there is not a lot he can do to make himself less alluring. Your best hope is another vampire coming to town.

Actually, this isn't a bad idea. Maybe ask your dearest one if he has any old friends who are single and might like the attention.

Or, hey, if you get really desperate, you could always *make* a new vampire. Head down to the gym and find yourself the vainest human there. You'll know him because he's stretching in front of the mirror and he's coated in fake tan. Tell him you've got a way he can keep those buns rock solid for eternity, without ever having to exercise again …

Although, given the risk to human life involved, this might be a bit irresponsible. Forget I said anything. Just put up with the admirers.

TIP 36
EX-VAMPIRE

💗

'I've been chatting up this gorgeous immortal and he's mentioned an ex-wife. He says it's nothing to worry about and they were only together for about 120 years. Will she be angry? Am I putting my life in danger by pursuing a vampire's man?'

Your life is in danger, regardless of whether you're making the moves on her former beau or not. Even if she isn't jealous, she is a predator – she's hungry and mean and she doesn't have a soul.

Although couldn't you say that about so many ex-girlfriends? I mean, when a guy gives me the speech about 'needing some time' and then three hours later I see him flirting with someone else, I've thought about cornering the new girl in a dark alley and biting her on the neck. Feelings can be hard.

Vampires can be pretty possessive, so if she isn't convinced it's over with this guy, then you could be in trouble. However, she is less likely to go straight for your jugular and is more likely, out of pride, to try to win him back first. Which gives you some time. Time you should spend inside your house, eating garlic, polishing silver and wording an eloquent apology to her.

It's his business, though. If their relationship didn't end well, he owes it to you to deal with her before getting involved with you. If the heart-to-heart method doesn't work, he'll need to employ the stake-to-heart method. Turn his vampire ex into an ex-vampire. Sounds extreme, but, hey, we know how dangerous exes can be. We've all been one.

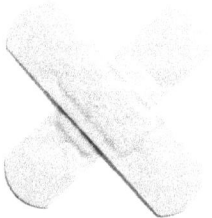

TALK TO THE ANIMALS

♥

'I've noticed black birds, huge moths and even bats flapping against windows whenever I talk to other guys. Is this my jealous vampire boyfriend's way of keeping an eye on me? And why are they always such creepy animals?'

In Bram Stoker's *Dracula*, the title character could change into a bat or a dog or even mist. I don't hold with this. Believing in vampires is one thing. Believing there can be a violation of the basic law of conservation of mass is quite another.

(This wasn't the only inconsistency in *Dracula*. Jonathan could not have found his way back to the castle after the confusion of his first trip there. Also, the characters' journal entries are unrealistically long – there is no way anyone would bother recording up to five pages per day, not when they had to write it all by hand. Even in the olden days. Apart from that, it's a pretty good book.)

Back to the question: a vampire can be born with or cultivate the ability to 'command' bats, dogs or any other animal and, to a degree, can 'inhabit' these animals. So it is possible for him to use animals to spy on you.

But if he wanted to spy on you, he'd be able to do it much

more covertly all by himself. Remember how many times he's suddenly appeared in your room? Even though you've specifically asked that he start knocking because he's already caught you twice with the tweezers in a delicate place.

If you were being unfaithful, he'd probably be able to tell just by looking into your eyes. So if it is him sending these animals to hassle you, then he's purposefully creeping you out, which is why he sends the creepy ones.

If he is doing this, he's a bit paranoid.

If he's not, you're a bit paranoid.

Either way, you guys are gonna have some bumps in the road if you don't see a professional about these trust issues. Therapy doesn't just help humans. It helps vampires too. Good luck.

MIRROR RULES

♥

'It's the old joke about vampires: if they can't see themselves in a mirror, how come their hair always looks so good? So what I want to know is, yeah, how come?'

Well, duh, he's just beautiful. Outrageously beautiful guys don't need mirrors. He doesn't have pimples that need squeezing and he doesn't get spinach caught in his teeth. He's completely forgotten how much a mortal needs a mirror, which is why he stares at you in such a fascinated way when you spend half an hour in front of it with a hair straightener. (And don't you wish he didn't. Hair doesn't straighten properly when it's embarrassed.)

Anyway, what everyone gets mixed up about it is that a vampire *can* see himself in a mirror. His reflection looks weird, though, like a 3D movie does when you're not wearing the glasses, except even foggier, so he's accustomed to hiding it. In fact he's spent a lifetime using his stealth and his ability to manipulate human perception to ensure he's never been seen in a reflective surface, and he's not going to let you ever see it.

So you won't catch him looking in a mirror, but you will catch him looking at you looking in a mirror. So embarrassing.

TIP 39
HAIR STYLING

♥

'While we're talking appearance, why won't he change his hairstyle? I mean, don't get me wrong: he's hot. But, like I keep telling him, he could look even hotter with something a bit more "on trend". Plus he'd look less like he'd escaped from the set of a period movie.'

Oh fashionable one, what you have to remember is that most vampires are basically really, really old people, and old people are bad at change. First of all, you should thank your lucky stars that it's his hair he refuses to change, and not, like so many really, really old men, his pants as well. And you need to recognise that he's not being resistant to change for no reason. His hair grows really, *really* slowly – almost not at all – unless he makes a great deal of effort to regenerate. Imagine how you'd feel if in order to grow out that two-centimetre blunt fringe you accidentally cut (I'm talking personal experience here), you had to go to ground for a period of six to nine months with a belly full of blood. You'd think twice about fooling with your style too.

Also, could it be that you're a little ungrateful? Chances are you fell for him because of that canopy of floppy, romance-novel hair atop his skull. So he'd better not get rid of it – he may need it to attract another girlfriend when you get bored of every other aspect of him as well.

Think about it. This relationship is meant to be the biggest, wildest, most romantic thing that's ever happened to you. If you're already getting impatient with his hair, then maybe you're not quite psychologically ready for eternal love.

Remember, there is an upside to his inflexibility. The loyalty he shows to his old hairstyle, he will also show in his relationship with you. And if you haven't already discovered it, it's a mental inflexibility only. Not physical. You're really a very lucky girl. Hell, you can't even see his hair in the dark.

TIP 40
PHANTOM BOYFRIEND

♥

'I think my friends and workmates are starting to doubt I have a boyfriend. He never drops in for lunch or picks me up at the end of the day, he never calls me when I'm with them and, most suspicious of all, there are no pictures of him in my Facebook albums. Trust me, they're looking. How do I stop them thinking I'm crazy?'

First of all, you need to help him understand how important these things are in maintaining a sense of normality. It doesn't just prevent your friends staging a we-think-your-boyfriend's-imaginary intervention; it also prevents him attracting attention for being a weird recluse, which wouldn't help his anonymity.

Fake a weekend away, and let him Photoshop some photos of the two of you against a bright tropical island sunshine background. And get him a phone, even though he doesn't need one to stay in touch, just so that he can send texts often enough to satisfy your buddies. Get him to send ones cancelling dates and asking stupid questions so they annoy you in a way that realistically simulates a regular relationship.

You also might want to pretend it's a long-distance love affair. Tell them he's moved out of town, and that he only gets to visit for very short periods of time. Then when you have one of those days when you're really tired, you can say it's because you were up all night 'talking on the phone'.

You should try not to care too much what they think anyway. If the relationship lasts the distance there will come a time when you will have to say goodbye to all of these people and not look back. You might move and stay in touch, but you won't be able to see them again. And you might want to shut down your Facebook account and just stick to email, as after this point not only will there be no photos of him in your albums, there'll be none of you either.

TIP 41
OFFICE PARTY

♥

'My office social club event is in two weeks and we're instructed to invite our partners. He says he'd do anything for me, so should I ask him to do this?'

No. You shouldn't.

The 'bring your partner' office party should be outlawed. Even if you're not dating a vampire, it is the most unnecessary, uncomfortable, relationship-straining night in your social calendar.

Your boy can handle it better than a regular mortal man, though. He's well practised at responding to the usual questions.

Question: 'So, how did you two meet?'

Answer: 'Through a mutual friend on a camping trip.'

Truth: He followed you for a few months before finally saving you from another vampire at midnight in open parklands.

Question: 'Have you lived around here all your life?'

Answer: 'Only since moving for work a few years ago.'

Truth: He hasn't *lived* here, or anywhere, for a couple of centuries. Technically, he's been dead since 1770.

Question: 'So what do you do to put food on the table?'

Answer: 'A little bit of IT work and some website design. Hence the tan.'

The truth: He bites his food to death and he doesn't use a table.

The difficulty is that you're going to have to learn the same lies so you don't contradict his story. Tricky.

And there are further precautions to take, if he does decide to come along. You'll have to arrive after dark, obviously, and you'll want it to be a dimly lit venue. Hopefully everyone else has had a drink by then. I'm sure you're not immune to his looks yet, but even so, you'll have forgotten how capable he is of making a whole roomful of jaws drop. But a little bit of low lighting and a couple of bottles of wine will give people something to blame for him looking so good.

Either tell people he's your designated driver or bring a little fresh blood at the bottom of a red wine bottle. Again, this is where dim lighting will help you out, because blood looks very 'full bodied' in a wine glass.

He'll need to avoid getting in any of the party snaps too. This will be the biggest strain on the both of you. If a snap-happy friend takes you by surprise, he may have to fake a sudden violent stomach upset and drop out of shot. Then you can both race off and be home before 9.30 pm. Which is the best possible result for an office social club event anyway.

DON'T TELL MY MOTHER

♥

'I don't live with my mother anymore, but we're very close, and I know she can tell there's something serious going on. Can I tell her about him without telling her the complete truth?'

For goodness' sake, don't even think about telling her the complete truth.

It's one of the golden rules – your mother should never know every detail about your significant other, even when you're dating a mortal.

For example, she never knew that your last boyfriend had a twenty-grand credit card debt and was dealing pot to get out of it, did she? She just knew he was a sweet boy who made her daughter smile. Well, sometimes he made you smile. Not when he called you to come and pick him up from the police station. That did not make you smile. Oh wow, thank goodness that relationship's over.

But my point is, your mum never needed to know any of that.

Rather than telling her about him, introduce him to her in person. He's very charming. She'll probably fall in love with him a bit herself.

She'll be able to see there's something extraordinary about him and, in her own time, she may even work it out. But don't spell it out for her. 'Vampire' belongs – along with 'testicles', 'threesome' and 'anal hemorrhage' – on a list of words you should never use in conversation with your mother.

The situation will get harder if, one day down the track, you decide to take the next step with this guy and join him in immortality. Most commonly, people move away and discontinue contact with home, but if you're close to your mother, this will be very difficult for you.

Here's my advice. If you reach this moment, first prepare by going out shopping with your mother to buy a dress for a special event. Make sure you also need to get matching shoes, underwear and make-up. You'll no doubt disagree on how short the dress should be, whether or not you'll wear your hair up, and whether or not nice girls wear stockings. By the end of the day you'll be ready to cut all ties.

YES, MRS VAMPIRE

♥

'He's going to introduce me to his mother and father! It's an honour, but they're not his real mother and father, are they? How are they connected and why do vampires "adopt" other vampires?'

Not all vampires gather in family groups.

Anti-social vampires are unlikely to put the effort into bringing a human back from the dead and feeding them their own blood, so do not end up 'making' family members.

Therefore, any vampire that is created will likely have a maker who wishes to mentor them through at least their first few years.

The family structure is dictated by 'who made who'. A vampire may refer to their maker as 'mother' or 'father'. If their 'father' has a partner, she will be referred to as 'mother', and vice versa.

The exception to this rule is if a vampire's creator takes the new vampire as a lover, in which case the vampire does not refer to their creator as mother or father. That would just be creepy.

So it's not a case of vampires adopting each other, rather they 'adopt' a human and give 'birth' to a vampire.

Sometimes vampires will gather in a family according to similar lifestyle choices – such as not feeding on humans (vampire vegetarianism) or living apart from human society (Amish vampires) or building a drug empire (who do you think invented methamphetamines?) – without any having made another. Then they will simply use the terms 'brother' or 'sister'. They will generally be loyal as though they were blood relatives. Loyalty is one of the few admirable qualities of the vampire race. They're pretty abhorrent apart from that, what with the killing and the feeding.

Not your guy, though, and hopefully not his parents, either, since you're off to visit them soon. I'm sure they won't kill you. No, really, you'll be fine. Off you go …

TIP 44
BROTHERLY LOVE

♥

'His brothers look at us really weirdly. Are they angry that he's dating a human?'

No, they're just hungry.

You clearly haven't been mixing with vampires for long enough to recognise that look. It says: 'You finished with that? Can I have some?'

They wouldn't dream of trying to steal a bite, of course. As you may have already gathered, vampires have a very strict system of 'dibs'. And you've been 'dibbed'. So you're safe. You're only at risk if some sort of powerful vampire Lord (I know, sounds melodramatic, but there are some vampires that call themselves that …) takes a fancy to you.

It probably won't happen. I mean, you're special, but you're not that special, right?

If it does happen, it probably means death, so it might be just the excuse you're looking for to make the leap into immortality, because then you have a better chance of negotiating with him, or at least living long enough to return to your beloved.

So don't comment on the way his brothers look at you, because they don't mean to, and don't complain if they avoid you on some days and go rushing off into the forest when they see you, because they're probably doing it for your own good.

LIKE A VIRGIN

♥

'He's had sex with a vampire before, but I haven't. How do I make our first time "special"?'

Here's how – by attempting to live through it.

Take a trip to your local hardware store, and put together some makeshift restraints out of chains and padlocks. It's not kinky, I swear. Well, no more so than planning sex with a vampire in the first place.

You wouldn't dream of sleeping with a new boyfriend without protection, and I can tell you that pregnancy and STIs have got nothing on bleeding to death in a violent fit of passion. Seriously, he can snap you like a twig. He can bite through you like you're butter. He can … sorry, am I ruining the sexy mood?

So chain him to the bed, if it's heavy enough, or the pot belly stove or the brick barbecue out back. Remember how strong he is. Don't chain him to the hot water heater, for example, because he'll probably damage it and it'll cost well over a grand to replace.

Scatter rose petals, sure. Light candles, that's nice. But don't forget the chains.

Even with him in restraints, he's still got a chance of hurting you. So keep garlic close at hand. No, it won't hurt him, but it might snap him out of it, kind of like the time you mentioned your mother during a session with your last boyfriend.

And finally, make sure he's well fed. If he hasn't slept in a long time that's better too, he'll be less likely to lose control. Well, no, he'll still lose control. Oh boy. Trust me, even with this long list of precautions you are about to experience the sort of passion that will blow every previous experience you've had out of the water. It will definitely be 'special'… although maybe not in the way you were expecting.

BREAKING UP

♥

'He's always trying to end our relationship. The first time I was devastated, but now I know that I only have to wait a few weeks and he'll come back and apologise. Still, it's starting to wear me out.'

Are you sure you're not loving the drama? Some ladies wait all their lives to be in a relationship that is intensely passionate, but with occasional breaks in which to 1) complain about men with their friends and 2) get some jobs done around the house.

For the rest of us, it's no way to live. Even though you say he always comes back, you must worry every time that this might really be the time he stays away.

The problem is that if he cares for you, he's going to feel certain that you're better off without him. No matter how happy a vampire is as an immortal, he's bound to have some issues about his own lack of soul, and how it was taken from him, and he wouldn't wish that on a human that he sees as good and pure.

The solution to relationship problems is generally as simple as telling someone how you feel. 'Hey, you've broken up with me ten times in six months and every time it hurts.

If you're so uncomfortable dating a mortal, I've half a mind to take matters into my own hands and go vampire.'

(That's just a threat, though! Don't actually get rid of your precious little soul on the off-chance you might love this guy who you've only spent a grand total of forty-eight hours with. That's something a crazy person would do. Remember that time your friend's boyfriend mentioned he liked tattoos and she turned up with his name on her lower back and then he ran a mile and she had to turn it into a flower-covered vine? It would be like that.)

Then tell him, 'Stop messing me round and get your shit together, buddy.' He'll get that, and it feels good to talk tough to a vampire.

DEAD BLOOD

♥

'Are all vampires so moody? He goes through long periods of being relaxed and pleasant, and then he'll spend a week being really intense and brooding. It's almost like he has a woman's hormonal cycle.'

You might find an all-important clue in the last part of your question.

Sounds to me as though your beloved is in sync with your cycle. Not because of any hormonal rhythms in his body, but because for one week a month, you smell as though you have blood to spare. Don't be grossed out; it's a beautiful, natural part of being a woman and he probably finds it very attractive. Too attractive, in fact. So he has to work a lot harder to control himself around you for about five days each month.

I'm surprised he hasn't bothered explaining all this to you. Maybe he's being a gentleman, or maybe he just figured you'd work it out yourself. But you didn't.

So in case you didn't work this out either, here's some important advice: at this time of the month, it's a good idea to keep clean and dispose of sanitary products carefully. No need to confuse his nose any more than necessary.

Although, it is said that 'dead blood' is no good for a vampire. That is, if he feeds on a dead person the blood will make him ill. Therefore, we can speculate that the kind of blood we're discussing here would be borderline toxic for him. Less like a glass of quality shiraz and more like a premix spirit in a can. Definitely only to be consumed if desperate. Ew.

TIP 48
WEANING HIM ONTO ANIMALS

❤

'He seemed so nice when I first met him. I just assumed he was one of those good vampires that fed off animals. Now I find out, three months into the relationship, that he is still drinking from humans. He claims he never kills them, though. Is he telling the truth? And is there anything I can say to him to change his ways?'

He could be telling the truth. It's possible for a vampire not to kill his victims, but it's really hard for a vampire to go on feeding in an area, undetected, when he leaves witnesses alive.

It's time for him to be weaned off human blood, and he knows it. You can't date the same species you eat.

You needn't nag him about it, but you should really revoke his invitation into your home until he can honestly tell you that he's made the change to animals. It's just common sense (not to mention a sign of self-respect) that he's not allowed to come over for dinner when you're potentially on the menu.

You can also help him out by telling him you believe in him and that you love him enough to wait for him while he's getting off the hard stuff.

And you can even participate in the weaning process by sewing some human costumes for the ill-fated animals to wear. Little overall-and-straw-hat farmer costumes to put on sheep, matching USA tracksuits for pigs, and some cute sequined club wear for stray cats. Just to make the transition easier for him.

ROMANTIC MEAL

♥

'Are you sure there's nothing else he can eat? It's just that, for once, I'd like to have a romantic meal together. I thought maybe black pudding, because it's made of blood, or a really rare steak.'

I know he will have explained this to you and that you already know the answer. Sadly, you're not going to get a different answer from me.

He consumes blood *only* and, more than that, it should be relatively fresh from the artery.

It's sweet of you to be thinking laterally like this but, really, how much vital life force do you think there is in a blood sausage?

Besides that, there are contaminants such as bread crumbs and heavy fats in a black pudding and in a rare steak there are contaminants such as, well, steak. He just can't eat that.

Find something else romantic to do together. You can still take walks beside the river at night, and you can listen to your favourite music while resting your head on his chest. But just forget about picnics and dinners, or having him lick cream off your shoulder. There's nothing romantic about the way he eats. He cannot use the nice silver, and he can't carry on a conversation about art-house cinema at the same time.

If it's really important to you, you can stage a romantic dinner and he can mime for you with miniature tea cups and bits of plastic fruit, like a doll's tea party, but don't blame me if he doesn't come back for more.

VALENTINE'S DAY

♥

'One of the nicest gifts I ever got was a basket of chocolates left on my doorstep. Since it's our first Valentine's together, is there something particularly delicious I could give him as a treat? Short of filling a Tupperware container with my own blood ...'

Yeah, nothing will compare to that.

One day, when you completely trust his self-control, you should do that. Leave the Tupperware container on his doorstep, though, and don't stick around to watch what happens next. Here's a clue: it'll be even more undignified than you were with those chocolates.

Given that we're working with a menu of blood only, you can either show your love through the effort taken, say by buying a fluffy bunny rabbit and feeding it rose petals for a few days prior, or by choosing the most delicious of animals, which is probably a pig. Pig's blood is the most similar to human blood. But it looks less adorable in a basket on his doorstep than the bunny would.

All edible gift ideas are going to be a bit tricky in your first year together, because he'd probably still prefer to keep his relationship with you separate from his ghoulish diet. So you might want to shelve the bunny rabbit idea until next year and – wow, I never expected to ever say this to anyone – perhaps the best gift really is a book voucher.

TIP 51
HE'S A LUSH

♥

'Does a relationship with a vampire mean a life of complete sobriety? I mean, he can't drink, can he? And it'd be weird to party knowing that he was always sober.'

A vampire generally likes to be sober. He prides himself on his quick reflexes and his ability to control any situation. It's bad enough for him that he ever has to sleep. So the last thing he wants is to get drunk knowing that it makes him vulnerable to a staking, or passing out and waking up in sunshine, or getting his eyebrows shaved off, which he finds particularly scary (see Tip 39: Hair styling).

Having said that, some vampires do imbibe, and it works the way you'd think it would: they drink the blood of an intoxicated person. (Or the blood of someone under the influence of drugs. Not that I'm endorsing the use of illegal substances. But vampires, well, so much of their lifestyle is already illegal – document forgery, livestock poaching, driving a vehicle while dead – why would they worry about breaking one more law?)

So the good news is that you can, theoretically, share a bottle of wine. And more good news, it involves you drinking the whole bottle by yourself. And the great news is that this means you're mildly anesthetised when he goes to DRINK IT STRAIGHT FROM YOUR NECK. Did I tell you the bad news? Yeah, it's that he DRINKS IT STRAIGHT FROM YOUR NECK. It doesn't appeal to me, but you two have fun. Did I mention that you should always drink responsibly?

Olden Day Role Play

♥

'I bought a book on the French Revolution, because that's around the period when he was born. I was wondering if he might like it if I got hold of some corsets and petticoats and we could role play from his old life. Some sort of peasant girl and nobleman scenario maybe. Perhaps with some sort of begging for mercy or something? How does that sound?'

Well, it sounds like a bit too much detail for me, but I'm sure your fella would love the offer. You might find he wants to reverse roles though. As in, he plays the peasant and you play the cruel, noblewoman lover who belittles him. Or maybe he'd like to play the noblewoman and you the guillotine master who he has to beg for mercy, hey, who knows? You know what they say about powerful men enjoying being humiliated during role play. I mean, I had a boyfriend once who … oh, no, that's right, too much detail. Sorry.

Anyway, it's a nice idea and even if you don't end up doing the dirty dress-ups thing, he'll be really touched you're taking the time to learn about his life and times. And it will better help you understand his references to the Scarlet Pimpernel and 'letting them eat cake'. And, no, neither of these are sex terms.

DOCTOR

♥

'I need to visit the GP to renew my pill prescription but I have a bit of an accidental bite on my neck. I know he'll notice and I'm worried he'll flag me as a potential domestic violence case. What can I tell him?'

I'm gonna assume you are on the pill for non-contraceptive reasons. There are no official statistics on it, but I don't think the pill offers complete protection when it comes to vampires. Perhaps a little garlic mixed into your lube would do a better job?

Maybe you're using the pill to clear up your skin. You've probably noticed it's even worse since you started getting 'accidentally' bitten more often. Losing blood can really weaken your immune system. While you're at the doctor's, get your blood checked as well. You could find you're a little low on iron. (Although, if your vampire boyfriend is experienced enough, he may be able to check your iron levels just by taste.)

The old turtleneck solution is all well and good until it gets over thirty degrees, then wearing a woolly ribbed skivvy will arouse suspicion that you are hiding something. (Under thirty degrees, it only arouses suspicion that you may be a beat poet.)

A good long-term solution is to tell your GP that you own a monkey. Or that you clean the house of someone who owns a monkey. Or that you work at the monkey house at the zoo. The important part is the monkey. Everyone knows monkeys are bitey little animals who turn on humans all the time.

Your doctor may ask what kind of monkey. Tell him it's a macaque (they're the most affordable) and tell him it's immunised, or he'll try and force you to take all sorts of rabies shots and antibiotics for the bite.

As for your vampire, you might want to start letting him 'accidentally' bite you in less conspicuous places than your neck. Trust me: it can be a lot of fun finding those places.

TIP 54
BITE CONCEALMENT

♥

'Where can I find a concealer that will cover a bite mark? Does one even exist?'

Look, I know getting bitten on the neck is part of the fantasy, but, like I said in the previous tip, you kids need to find ways of putting bite marks in places that can be hidden by hair or clothing. Try the back of the neck, the upper arm or just above the hip-bone.

Also, be very careful. No matter how self-controlled he's been so far, you both need to remind yourselves how hard it is for him to stop once he gets a taste of blood.

He's essentially programmed to drink until you're dead. Always approach biting as the potentially lethal activity it is and make sure you both feel prepared to make it happen safely.

If you insist on letting him plant those dirty great big fangs right below your ear, you can purchase heavy-duty cover-up from specialist make-up stores. I'm talking about that skin-coloured putty that make-up artists use to create fake wounds on the world's most beautiful people. Just smear the putty into the holes and then powder the affected area. But don't get caught in heavy rain or your patch-up job will come apart at the seams.

MENDING THE PUNCTURES

♥

'Does aloe vera work on fang holes? I need this one to clear up fast cos I have to wear an evening dress to a black-tie event next week.'

Don't call them fang holes. Love bites sound so much nicer.

Imagine if I'd called this book *Fang Holes: 101 tips on getting fang-holed*, that wouldn't have exactly flown off the shelves, would it? Well, no, you're right, it does have a bit of a ring to it, but I think people would be picking it up for the wrong reasons.

Right, so … I'm sure aloe vera will help your bites.

The problem is that a vampire's teeth partially cauterise a wound on contact. What that means is the edge of the bite is sealed – so you lose less blood at skin level – but, as you may have already noticed, it dramatically slows the healing process.

In fact, these wounds can scar badly and may never disappear.

There are creams that can be purchased specifically to reduce scarring, but they're expensive. Worth it in the long run, though, if you're hooked on the fangs.

Hey, while you're at the chemist, look into getting yourself a couple of little disposable syringes. That way you can carefully extract a little taste of your blood for his pleasure, without marking yourself before a big event. And don't act all grossed out by the syringe suggestion! Honestly! You're the one that's getting fang-holed, you kinky princess.

No more biting questions, please.

DECAPITATION

♥

'How exactly does one decapitate a vampire? I'm only asking as a safety precaution. I'm not planning on hurting my fiancé at all, even though he's been disappearing a lot lately, for long periods of time, and he did mention that an old, female friend was in town ... It couldn't hurt for him to see I have the equipment at hand, could it?'

There are a couple of questions to address here.

Before we deal with the how-to's of a beheading, let's address the jealousy issue, shall we? You'll forgive me, but reading between the lines, you sound like you could be a bit of a psycho-fiancée. Are you even engaged or have you just taken to calling him your fiancé ever since he, jokingly, called you 'a good little housewife' or something equally meaningless?

Let's give you the benefit of the doubt and say that you are engaged. And if he has sworn to marry you, you can only give him the benefit of the doubt and trust that he will keep his promise.

I can't stress this enough. You have agreed to an engagement with a member of the enchanted undead, whose past is filled with centuries of dark secrets. You can't know everything, so you just have to trust him.

You are right to worry if there are frequent disappearances and if there's an 'old friend' in town, but not for the reason you think. He's just as likely to be protecting her, protecting you from her or protecting the rest of the community from her. He's so used to living secretly, it probably hasn't occurred to him to fill you in on whatever secret battle is going down.

So give him the benefit of the doubt. If you truly believe you're being played, then shut the relationship down, but don't pack a duffel bag full of beheading tools and follow him home. Save the duffel bag full of beheading tools in case he really is trying to protect you from *her*.

And if you do come across her, here's the process: a stake to the heart, to paralyse your victim. It will require a great deal of strength to get the stake deep enough. There will be some violent thrashing and some awful noises before she goes quiet. If you're a bit angry at her, it will help.

Then you will need to summon even more strength for the beheading itself. If you can get your hands on a power saw, you will be glad of a little extra grunt. Vampires' necks are seriously as hard as tree trunks. It's also a great idea to invest in some safety goggles and protective clothing, because things can get messy.

I know, this doesn't sound like it does in the stories. It's really hard work and really gross. You're really gonna need a shower afterwards … to wash away the mess … and the awful memories.

TIP 57
SLAYERS AND OTHER HATERS

♥

'Do slayers exist? What am I meant to do if I meet one?'

Slayers do exist and they're not quite as adorable as Buffy. They are weird, reclusive, nomadic types, not unlike the creatures they hunt.

Let's face it: it takes a pretty fanatical character to devote their life to ridding the planet of so-called abominations. In fact, you can group slayers in with TV evangelists, KKK members and cosmetic surgeons as the sorts of obsessives you wouldn't want to get stuck in a lift with.

You're not likely to get stuck in a lift with a slayer, though, because they don't often bother with tall buildings. They concentrate more on parks, alleyways, docklands and under bridges. And they're much more concentrated in areas such as Eastern Europe, where the vampires are also more concentrated.

If you do meet a slayer, don't confront him, you will only draw his attention to the presence of a vampire in the area.

Also, there are some really awful vampires out there, so it's great if the slayer can take out a couple of the bad ones.

All you can really do is warn your beloved and stick close by him, so that if something goes down, you can throw yourself in his path as a human shield. Slayers hate to kill humans, so this will buy him a second or two, which is enough time for a vampire to get away. It will really endear you to your lover, too. They don't have their lives saved often. Although, can you call it 'saving his life' if he's already dead?

TIP 58
VAMPIRE-SAFE YOUR HOME

♥

'I want him to live with me in my place, but he seems reluctant to move in. Is my home not safe for him?'

Your home won't be safe for *you*, if he moves in. Why? Because it's now got a vampire in it. He's not the safest creature to live with, even if he does love you. Plus his presence makes the house a target for anyone who wishes him harm.

He's probably resisting the move for your own sake.

If you're keen to convince him, though, you can start by making some changes at home, to make the place more vamp-friendly.

Replace any open fires with wall heaters. Better for the environment, and less chance of accidental fire, which could burn his pretty self up. Make sure at least one room in the house has heavy-duty block-out curtains. Don't scrimp on quality. No chinks of light should get through.

Get rid of any 'stakey' items you have around the house – skis, wooden stools, giant novelty mixing spoons. You'd be surprised how many items make him nervous. For example, large timber picture frames look to him like four splintery stakes, all ready to go when the slayer breaks in. Remove these items from the house or, if you're not ready to throw them away, lock them up in a shed or basement.

(In fact, if you do have a basement, you might prefer to use it for his den, because then you don't need the block-out blinds. Make sure you double check all the vents and such to make sure there's nothing that can be wrenched away by an enemy to suddenly bathe the basement in light.)

Leave a nice big space for his coffin. If it turns out he doesn't have one, great, you can wheel your sewing machine out of the shed and set up in that spot again. (Which would be a relief; the sewing machine really does look a lot cuter than a coffin.)

TIP 59
MUST LOVE DOGS

♥

'I've always owned dogs, and want to get a pet for our new home together. Is he going to feel tempted around my dog like he is around me?'

He is. Frankly, it'll only be a matter of time before one bites the other.

The dog will smell a little less delicious to him than you, but he won't have as much sentimental attachment to it, so it would just be a matter of time until his blood-sugar levels* got low …

Remember, it's only his love for you that prevents him getting stuck right in every time he hears your heart beat.

If you must own a pet, consider a cat. For two reasons: cats are smaller and more nimble so will stand a slightly better chance of evading him if he makes a grab for them. They might shoot far enough under the house or along a tree branch to give him the moment he needs to remember that – like circus animals, your friend's budgie and your parents – this is something he promised you he wouldn't eat.

Also, cats are better than dogs, because if he does accidentally take a bite, you won't be quite as sad.

---

* Vampires actually use the phrase 'blood-blood levels'.

FLAMMABILITY

♥

'We've been looking for a place to live and he's being really fussy. I thought it was just fictional vampires who liked to live in big, old stone mansions with bad lighting and, more importantly, no walk-in robes. How can I convince him to ditch that cliché and move into this nice, new weatherboard cottage I've found?'

Now, now, don't be a bully over this. Finding the right house is much more important to him than it is to you, because it may keep you both alive.

For a start, your fella's probably lost a friend to fire and has learnt a lesson about weatherboards. When a vampire sleeps during the day (and, yes, he does a certain amount of this to heal and build his strength) he is vulnerable to attack. If his house is made of wood, it's easy for someone to attack by burning it down with your paramour inside.

If he is burnt to ashes, he cannot regenerate. If he escapes with burns, he will have a lot more sleeping to do before he's healthy enough to rebuild the walk-in robes and where's he going to sleep now the house is burnt?

He will also be concerned about you living in a wooden house. You are *as*, if not *more*, flammable than him. If the house burns down, you'll be burned along with him. And if you're lucky enough to be out at the time, you're still going to have trouble getting your bond back.

So that's why he's keen to find something built of cold stone and why he will want to keep it so sparsely furnished.

The rest of his choices are, just as you suspected, your boyfriend being a cliché. He wants to live in a mansion on a hill so that he can pretend it's one of the many fine houses in his real-estate portfolio from his previous life as a duke. Vampires are much more status obsessed and boastful about real estate than you'd realise. That's what you get when someone doesn't have a soul. Or lives in Sydney.

HOUSEWORK ROSTER

♥

'Why doesn't he help more with the household chores? Is it, as he says, because cleaning products will melt his immortal flesh?'

Cleaning products will remove traces of dirt and grime from his skin and leave a fresh, citrusy odour, just as they would with any other hard surface.

Nothing short of hydrochloric acid will melt his flesh. So, if necessary, threaten him with this in order to get him on board with the old roster system. If you can't get your hands on any hydrochloric acid, use those big baby blues and a calm voice to explain to him how it's going to be.

He understands that the chores need to be done by someone, of course. Vampires generally like their surroundings to be clean, tidy and with a fresh, citrusy odour.

Don't be put off by his initial resistance. Remember, he's spent many centuries manipulating others to get what he wants and it's only been in the last few decades that people have considered the possibility that housework might not be exclusively women's work. But it's very important to establish housework equality straight off the bat. Remember, this relationship could last *forever*. Which is a long time to be picking up somebody's dirty socks.

TIP 62

GENTLEMEN'S GROOMING

❤

'My least favourite thing about him is his fingernails. I could swear they change length every day! I wish he'd just keep them cut short.'

Consider yourself lucky. I once had a boyfriend who kept just the one fingernail long and openly referred to it as his 'nose-picking' nail. He could at least have pretended it was for playing guitar or defusing bombs or something.

Anyway, well done noticing the nail thing. Unlike most of the vampire's body, which remains unchanged and only regenerates in the case of injury, his fingernails experience regular growth. Like a vampire's teeth, their growth is triggered by his need to feed.

A vampire who is deliberately starving himself will grow extremely long nails and pronounced teeth. He will also exhibit increasingly aggressive behaviour. Sounds lovely, doesn't it? So why would vampires do this? Well, sometimes immortality just bores you crazy.

Give your beau a not-so-subtle hint by buying him a nice manicure set, and remember that the creepy fingernails are just one more reason you want to keep him well fed.

HOUSEHOLD SAFETY

♥

'What happens if I have an accident at home and start bleeding? Will this put me in danger from him?'

If we're talking about a small injury – a paper cut or insect bite, for example – you shouldn't have to worry.

If it's a bit bloodier – say you slice yourself with a kitchen knife or graze your knee in the driveway – exercise caution. Don't wave the injured limb in his face. Cover it and move quickly to the bathroom, being careful not to leave a tantalising little trail behind you. If you notice he's looking a little crazy-eyed, move even more quickly to the bathroom. And lock the door.

If there's truly any danger, he should have the good sense to run outside and not come back for a few minutes. By the time you move in together he should have mastered his thirst for your blood.

In fact, when it comes to really serious injuries, his presence is actually something of an insurance policy. Sure, a small cut will make him freak out a little but if you ever fatally injure yourself, Doctor Fangs can step in and, as a last resort, resurrect you.

Don't use the old 'fatal injury' ploy to hurry him into that before he's ready, though. Turning someone he loves into a vampire is a high-pressure job as it is, without the additional stress of being taken by surprise. You could end up the boring kind of dead, or still human but really, really sore.

TIP 64
INSIDE A VAMPIRE'S MIND

♥

'Why does he sit and stare at nothing rather than talk to me? Am I so boring that it's more interesting to look at the wall for five hours? It freaks me out. Sometimes he sits so still I think he's dead!'

Um, first of all, you've forgotten something … he *is* dead. Well done. I mean, just cos someone walks and talks and kisses you and moves in with you, doesn't mean they're necessarily alive.

Second of all, he's not staring at nothing. Perhaps he's watching the shadows cast by the moon, or listening to conversations that your neighbour's neighbours are having, or entertaining himself with one of many centuries of classic memories. Like that time he and a friend dressed up as women and danced in the chorus line of a West End musical. Or the time he lived undetected for three months in the back shed of a major world politician. Or the time he met another vampire in the cargo hold of a ship and only after three weeks of talking did they realise they went to school together back in 1814. Good times.

Sitting still for five hours may be inconceivable to you, but a vampire experiences time in a very different way to a mortal. Despite being able to move extremely quickly when necessary, he enjoys spending long periods moving slowly or not at all. His senses are so keen and his mind is always so alert that it is acutely pleasurable for him to be still and absorb the sight, sounds and smells around him.

If, one day, you get to experience this yourself, you will understand how he can spend hours on end just silently drinking it all in. In fact, in the first few weeks of being a vampire, you're likely to resemble some sort of experimental drug user, wide-eyed and unable to speak except for the occasional spaced-out question such as: 'Did the wind always sound like this?', 'Does time ever get lonely?' and 'Have you ever really looked, just looked, at your hands?'

TIP 65
THE DOOR IS ALWAYS OPEN

♥

'Now that we live together, can he invite other vampires inside? Or is it still only me who can do that?'

The good news is that you, as the human of the house, are the only one with that power, so you can rest assured that there will be no surprise vampire guests.

However, your immortal beloved is likely to be much better than you at recognising evil types, so it wouldn't hurt to consult him when choosing whether to invite someone in.

If your lover wants to invite his undead mates into the house, he will have to ask you to do the formal welcome for him, which feels a bit tragic for both parties.

A manipulative woman might use this to her advantage. 'Of course I'll invite your friends in, if you agree that loving someone means getting them a Cherry Ripe whenever they want it, even if they want one at 2 am every night of the week.' But I'm sure you're not such a mercenary person.

The perfect solution is to take a garage, bunker or shed and convert it into a vampire lounge. Then he can take the guys straight there, without your permission, to play poker or talk about girls or whatever it is they do … I hate to admit it, but even I can't pretend to know what men do in their sheds.

TIP 66
VAMPIRE MASSAGE

♥

'Does he like a ... you know ... a foot rub ... after a hard night? Because he comes home tense and I want to help him relax.'

Oh, come on, everyone likes a foot rub after a hard day. There are only three times people don't like foot rubs: when they have an odour issue; when they're overdue for some corn removal; and when they've painted their toenails with glitter polish and they don't want anyone to know they like glitter.

The problem is that you're probably not strong enough to give him a foot rub. While his skin is sensitive enough to notice even the lightest touch of the tiniest feather, his muscles are rock solid. It'd be like trying to squeeze the tension out of a concrete block.

Try giving him a back rub instead, because then you can stand on his spine and walk up and down on it. Maybe jump up and down a little. Even still, it's not going to feel like much to him, but he'll appreciate the effort.

Now, just in case 'foot rub' was a euphemism, I'll simply say that yes, you can give him a 'foot rub' and it will relax him. But definitely don't jump up and down on it, because it's not technically a muscle. Just normal pressure will do, but make sure he's got something other than you to bite down on, in case it's a really good … 'foot rub'.

TIP 67
OLD HABITS

♥

'He told me once we'd moved in together he'd stop sleeping in a coffin. But he keeps disappearing and guess where I find him? Am I fighting a losing battle?'

Even if you win the battle, are you sure it's worth the casualties? Every time you spring him curled up in his special place, you make him feel a bit less certain that this vampire–human relationship-thing is working out.

Not that I'm saying you should compromise your own beliefs just to avoid breaking up, but how much do you truly believe that he should sleep in a bed? (If that's even where you're trying to get him to join you. For all I know, you could be settling down for your sleepy times in the bath or on the floor of the pantry, in which case, I don't think you've got a leg to stand on when you're criticising the coffin.) Are you trying to pretend he's not a vampire?

He's obviously been sleeping in a coffin for a long, long time and even if he wanted to, he'd probably find the habit hard to break. Anyway, it seems like he doesn't want to. Trust me, he knows what he's doing when he 'sleepwalks' over for a sneaky nap in the satin.

If you ask me – which you did – it's time to stop asking him to change. Let him know you're okay with him sleeping that way, and then get okay with it. Maybe try the coffin yourself, just in case you take to it. I can categorically report, having lain in a coffin (a few times) and slept in a bath (once), that a coffin would not be the worst place to sleep.

GOTHIC CHIC

♥

'It's not just the coffin. It's the human skull, the candles in wine bottles, the dusty hundred-year-old portraits he puts on every surface. How do I explain to him that his taste in home decoration is just a bit … creepy?'

Oh, babe. His taste in home decoration is creepy? What about your taste in men? He's as much of a horror–show as that human skull is. Really, so long as your house contains an accursed soul who walks the Earth for all eternity, it doesn't matter how many funky throw rugs and vases of painted sticks you buy from Freedom, you're still, essentially, living in a crypt.

As with all home decoration arguments, you need to remind yourself that the most important thing you can put in your house is someone you love. I think that's a saying, I might have just made it up. But it's true! You've got a gorgeous goddamned vampire living *in your house* and what's more he likes you enough to share his most precious ornaments with you.

Now, given these ornaments are *truly* precious, maybe this sensational collection of gothic treasures should be kept together in a single room. Maybe a room that you can shut the door on so there's no chance of them being broken or stolen. Then you can go in and really appreciate them in peace and quiet, say, once or twice ... a year ...

But if this doesn't fly with him, remind yourself that he doesn't have the *worst* taste you've ever encountered. He could be bringing with him one of those mechanical singing fish or a life-sized promotional cardboard cut-out of Angelina Jolie from *Tomb Raider*'s DVD release or just a weird, old-sock smell, like some of the other guys you've dated.

TIP 69
VAMPIRE PSYCHIATRY

♥

'I've moved in with my vampire boyfriend and discovered he's a bit of a clean freak. In fact, I think he might have OCD. Can vampires suffer from mental illness?'

If it came down to a clinical diagnosis, any vampire could be considered mentally ill – the sneaking around, the daytime sleeping and, of course, the constant drive to kill.

They're not mentally ill, though, they're just vampires. In their own way, they're physiologically perfect in the brain area – they don't suffer from chemical imbalances, hormonal disturbances or deterioration of the brain cells.

However, as we already know, their strengths are amplified. So if one of their strengths is noticing when spice jars aren't straight, then you end up seeing some obsessive behaviour.

Explain to him that he's not normal – he knows this already, so it won't hurt his feelings to hear it again – and then ask him if he finds your messiness 'charming' or 'revolting'. If he still finds you adorable when he's picking your undies up from the bathroom floor, then congratulations, you may've not only found yourself the love of your life but also a permanent, perfectionist, live-in housekeeper.

If a coffee table strewn with magazines or a sink full of takeaway containers makes him unable to stand the sight of you, then you both need to sit down and work it out. Try to make more of an effort to keep your things in order and then he can be introduced to 'low-grade clutter' one baby step at a time. Who knows, he might end up hiding bottle caps under the sofa cushions too one day.

LAND BARON

♥

'I've just found out he's got a house in Rome, which he bought in the nineteenth century. How can he own property when he's not even human? I mean, according to the law, the owner couldn't still be alive after two hundred years, right?'

Vampires are very good at working the law to their advantage. He has probably engaged a solicitor to transfer ownership to his grandson of the same name. This way, he keeps the property in his name generation after generation.

Given the ease with which degrees can now be obtained online, he may even act as his own solicitor. (Ask him how many professions he's qualified for. He's quite possibly a lawyer, a doctor, a mechanical engineer and a reiki practitioner. He may even be a candlestick maker.)

Not only are they good at manipulating the law, they are brilliant with money, which is important when you want to live well without working. Small amounts of cash, received as gifts or stolen from victims, can be invested wisely to reap great rewards. Which means he can afford even the most expensive internet degrees, such as dentistry and game-show modelling.

TIP 71
NIGHT COURT

💔

'If he gets arrested for, say, trespassing, what is the best course of action? Run away or stay and face the legal process?'

You are asking me that question as though you would have any say in the decision, when in fact there'd be no discussion. He'd be long gone before you even heard anything had happened. Vampires don't sit in jail cells and turn up to court just to keep up appearances. They disappear.

He's unlikely to get caught, though. The best thing about being good at disappearing is that you can do it before the police arrive, if they are even called. He's too cold to set off heat sensors, too careful to trigger motion sensors, and if he intends to commit a crime, his victim's usually dead before they can call the police. Especially if his victims are livestock, because cows and chickens don't call the police when they notice something suspicious.

Your only concern is if your beloved gets in trouble with the vampire authorities. Not that they have police or courts exactly, but there are some ruling vampires who have adopted their positions based on their own superior powers and who will punish those who they see posing a threat to themselves or the secrecy of the vampire community.

To avoid trouble among his own, he needs to give them anything they ask for and just generally, and I quote, 'not be a dickhead vampire'. If he can manage this, he shouldn't have any problems. But if he can't, he should know that in this case it's better to stay and face the music, because he can't outrun them. Even if he could, you can't, and they're not above punishing someone by hurting the person they love.

TIP 72
MAIL-ORDER VAMPIRE

♥

'I can't speak for all of your other readers, but I'm here at Tip 72 and I still haven't even met a vampire. Are there any online dating sites?'

Take a pen and put a big fat cross through the idea of looking for a vampire online. 'I'm a vampire' is one of the three most common lies on the internet, along with 'I'm thirteen years old' and the declaration that one is 'laughing out loud'. There hasn't been a LOL that was genuinely a LOL since the guy who invented the internet noticed that no less than twenty-four hours later there was already porn on it and mirthfully slammed his hand down on the L and O keys. He didn't mean 'laughing out loud'; it was just a coincidence. Anyway, interesting bit of trivia for you.

You may find a vampire online, but he's there hunting for future meals, so he's more likely to say 'I'm thirteen years old' than 'I'm a vampire'. Unless he's pretending to be someone pretending to be a vampire, so that he can meet another person pretending to be a vampire and pretend to meet them for dinner, but really meet them *for* dinner, if you know what I mean.

No, if you're looking to widen your search, then unfortunately you can't do it from the comfort of your home office. The only way is to pack your bags and travel the world looking for love. This is an expensive way to hunt for vampire love, and thus a last resort. But it's worth it, because even if you don't get completely lucky, you may get half-lucky and have a holiday fling with a human who's just fun enough to take your mind off vampires for a little while. If that's possible.

TRAVEL AGENCY

♥

'As luck would have it, I've been saving for a holiday and have time off work coming up. Where should I go and how much will it cost?'

Your biggest cost is your airfare. You won't need much money for accommodation, sightseeing or drinking. You'll basically be staying in your budget motel and walking the streets every waking hour.

The only other large expense will be relocation costs, but you only have to consider this if your vacation is a complete success, so we'll get to that later …

Before you head to your travel agent, you'll want to decide on a shortlist of destinations, and you may want to invent a good reason why you want to go to Transylvania, Slovenia and anywhere else you'd struggle to place on a map. Vampire hotspots are cities in and around Eastern Europe – look for densely populated areas with high crime rates and plenty of dilapidated buildings. The vampire knows he can escape detection in such places. If you hear superstitious tales from the locals about where vampires are reputed to reside, start your search there, because chances are they're right.

Remember to stay safe. Just like back home, vampires are hungrier for blood than they are for love and you are particularly vulnerable when in an unfamiliar place with limited ability to speak the language. Worst of all, a vampire who decides he wants you only has to pay at the front desk to get an invite across the threshold of your very cheap hotel. So the trick is to be sure you are somewhere sufficiently well lit or crowded for a first meeting and don't stay out till dawn, because that's when the desperate vampires are out trying to find someone to follow home. Just like with real men.

TIP 74
DON'T DISCRIMINATE

♥

'Are the vampires different in Transylvania? I mean, are they the kind of vampires I should be dating?'

You shouldn't be dating any kind of vampire, really, so what does it matter where they're from?

Sure, it might be easier to maintain a relationship with someone of a similar cultural background, but the fact that you're after a vampire at all means you're not exactly looking for the easy path to love.

The only risk you run in Transylvania is of meeting a really old vampire (see Tip 30). But, hey, they're still charming, and they're the classic version of the vamp: heavily accented English; tall, dark and handsome; Catholic background. You might even find one who still flinches at the sight of a cross.

But there's no need to make Transylvania your only stop. Consider places such as Morocco, Delhi, Cape Town, Los Angeles or Hong Kong. Vampires come from every cultural and religious background. Perhaps you'll be lucky enough to meet a Buddhist vampire. Well, ex-Buddhist. He can give away his assets, live in a cave and spend a lot of time being silent, but he fails on the 'not killing any living thing' rule every time.

PHRASEBOOK

♥

'How much of the language do I need to speak to court a foreign vampire?'

You won't need much, because any sociable and sensible vampire has learnt the basics of the major world languages. He may have spent a decade or two living in an English-speaking city just for kicks.

If for some reason he doesn't speak any English, you will still be able to make a connection, just by using gestures and facial expressions. Some might even consider this the most fun way to do it.

You may as well learn a few phrases, just for the hell of it. Pick things that are going to sound cute in your foreign accent, like 'Hello, it is nice to meet you' and 'I am happy to be seeing your city'.

If you are good at learning languages, you can throw in some more provocative lines like, 'What are you drinking tonight?' and 'I wasn't planning on sleeping till the morning'. As a precaution, you should also learn how to say, 'I keep a wooden stake in my handbag'. You both still know he could overpower you if he wanted, but it lets him know that if he's looking for sustenance he should look elsewhere. After all, a modern girl carries protection.

TIP 76

PEN PALS

♥

'Can we maintain a long-distance relationship or will he stray when I'm not nearby?'

I've always felt that if you're going to have a long-distance boyfriend, you may as well just invent a make-believe boyfriend because you get just as few cuddles but don't have to worry about him meeting someone else. But I'm a very impatient person, and you may be better at waiting for things than me.

Don't do it unless you know it's for a limited time. And definitely don't let him convince you that it could work long-distance for your entire life. A lifetime is nothing for him, but it's all you've got.

As for any loyalty concerns, your average vampire is utterly capable of maintaining a faithful relationship from afar. If anything, he's too good at it and may forget how differently time passes for humans. By the time he remembers to come and visit, you may have started wearing big, beige, nanna knickers and watching *Antiques Roadshow*.

If you think you might have found the real thing, you should get stuck in properly, in the same city, as soon as possible. If it doesn't work out, at least you found out sooner rather than later. And if he turns out to be the love of your never-ending life, why wait years to get started? What a shame to become a vampire in big, beige, nanna knickers …

RELOCATION, RELOCATION

♥

'Should I move to him or should he be the one to relocate?'

There are arguments for both. He is better at languages, forging documents for himself and has less or no family to say goodbye to. But, as a human, you can adapt more easily to a new place and it's much easier for you to travel, given that you do it in a seat rather than a box.

Do you live in the sort of place he could move to? Would he have plenty of access to wildlife and is there enough going on at night so that he wouldn't get terribly bored? If so, it is the easiest option. Because if you move to where he lives you're going to struggle to get yourself established. You'll find it hard to get work, you'll initially be very lonely and when it comes to extending your visa, you can't just marry him for citizenship, because he doesn't really exist.

There is one big plus to you moving, and that's that you'll never have to introduce him to your parents, never have to take him to any excruciating family dinners and never have your friends ask why he doesn't come out with you more often.

Perhaps this is the best option. After all, he's got all the time in the world to teach you the language and forge your citizenship documents …

CABIN OR CARGO?

💙

'What's involved in a successful vampire relocation? Is he going to have his own passport?'

If he doesn't have a passport, he can get hold of one. There are places you can get one for the right price and they're the sort of places that are open at night.

He shouldn't need one, though, because he won't travel through normal channels.

It would be possible to carefully structure a travel itinerary around the different time zones so that he was travelling in darkness only. But then he runs the risk of flight delays into the daylight hours.

He could take a cruise, except that might take weeks and it would be hard to find enough non-human creatures to keep the hunger away. It takes nearly as much energy to catch a seagull as the energy you get from feeding on one. It's a recipe for disaster: hungry vampire, captive human population. You're just asking for a relapse.

No, he needs to travel as cargo.

Once upon a time, he would have just snuggled down in a big wooden box, but in today's security-conscious climate there are multiple scans performed on baggage and chances are quarantine would be called when the human skeleton showed up on the scanner screen. Bones are strictly a 'to be declared' material.

So he needs to travel in a coffin, as a body returning home. The paperwork's a nightmare, but once he's set up your home address as a funeral home (on paper only) and forged some documents to explain who his body belonged to, it should go off without a hitch.

If you find the thought of him trapped in that tight space for twenty-four hours with nothing to do and not even enough room to scratch himself, remember that you've been in exactly the same position, except that in your case, it was called 'the economy cabin'.

Non-invasive procedures

♥

'What advice can you offer on maintaining one's youth? We've made the decision to give it another few years before going eternal, but I don't want people to start asking if I'm his mother.'

I'm not the best person to ask about looking after your appearance. I believe that if people are talking about how old you are then it's because you're not giving them anything more interesting to talk about. Consequently, I have spent very little time studying under-eye cream and a great deal of time making loud pronouncements at dinner parties on controversial topics.

Anyway, what's the big deal if you're twenty-one and people think you look thirty-one? Thirty-one year olds can be attractive too and, besides, who's looking at your wrinkles when you're saying such audacious things about child prostitution?

As for remaining youthful, the two things I do know that take years off your appearance are staying out of the sun and being in love – so you're pretty much nailing it right now. Oh, and becoming a vampire, naturally, but you've wisely decided to put that off.

I commend you on your patience. A lot of girls are in this as much for the immortality as the vampire himself, but your humanity is a precious gift, and it's great that he's happy for you to enjoy a few more years of it.

There is nothing wrong with you growing old gracefully with him by your side, eternally young. Think about the elderly couples you know: inside that old man, there's a younger man, looking out at his old wife, still loving her. And your vampire is already much older than that old man. Much, much older.

Well, that's my advice. If that helps, I'm pleased. But if what you were looking for was a list of cosmetics recommendations, maybe just head to the beauty counter at your nearest department store.

TIP 80
PREMATURE AGEING

♥

'But I don't want to look like some sort of cougar cliché! I don't even like that TV show! I need to "age him up". Will small amounts of sunlight make him look a few years older?'

It's an ingenious idea – to sun-weather him for a more mature look. But it's not safe. It's hard to predict how quickly he will burn, and if it's a high-UV day, he might suddenly go up like a piece of magnesium over a match.*

Besides, it'll only take a good meal and a day's rest and he'll have completely rejuvenated, virtually before your eyes, meaning you'd have to do daily sunshine sessions. Time consuming.

There are less dangerous ways to add a few years to his life, if he's keen to do it for you. The best one is what I like to call the Mr Sheffield Touch, which has nothing to do with marrying your nanny and everything to do with faking up some sophisticated-looking grey cobwebs into the hair at his temples. You can use stage make-up, but it's better to

---

* I know. In Tip 11, I said that the sunlight couldn't make him burst into flames. That's still true. Forgive me for being melodramatic. He won't burst into flames. He will however make anguished noises from the pain of the sun searing into his immortal flesh. So don't do it.

get some bleach and grey hair dye. And maintain, maintain, maintain – grey hair with dark roots looks so weird.

It used to be that you could make a vampire look older by simply dressing him in cardigans and encouraging him to sit down a lot. Unfortunately, that look has been adopted of late by fashionable younger men, who like nothing better than to wear cardigans and sit down a lot. I'm looking at you, Josh Thomas.

FREE DRINKS

♥

'Does he really not want me to lose my soul, or is he just keeping me human so he can drink my blood?'

Oh, God, what a horrible thought. It is also a ridiculous thought, because no matter how delicious your blood is, it wouldn't be worth the effort of a relationship with a human just to get a little suck now and then. The love bites he gives you are part of a complex loving relationship, not him thinking of you as some sort of mini bar.

As I've already explained, it troubles a vampire to fall in love with a mortal. He doesn't want to lose you after only eighty years, but he can't bear the thought of turning you into a monster either. If he says he doesn't want you to lose your soul, he means it. So don't push him too hard.

If you pressure him into changing you before he's comfortable with it, he will always look at his handiwork with regret. I remember when I made my boyfriend shave me an undercut and he just couldn't bear how bad he'd made me look … oh, no, that wasn't me, that was Keanu Reeves and Martha Plimpton in *Parenthood* … Well, still, you get my point.

Proposing to Him

♥

'If he's 200 years old, will it blow his old-world mind if I ask him to marry me?'

He knows that the world has moved on from the way things were done when he was born. He is living in it, after all. The world has changed since you were born, too, and you've managed to stay up-to-date.

So it won't blow his mind. Unless he really, really wants to get married and just hasn't worked up the nerve to ask you, or really, really doesn't want to, in which case his normally placid face will break out into a look of nervous shock.

It is nice for him to think that you are mindful of his beliefs and upbringing, but he knows that you are a woman of your time and expects you to behave as such. So propose away.

I'm sure he won't mind if you want to keep your name, either. His last name probably isn't his birth name anyway, he'll have made a few changes along the way.

Hey, why don't you both invent a new last name to commemorate the marriage? Something like Mr and Mrs Fangsalot? Or Bloodslington? Or Jolie-Pitt?

TIP 83
LEGALLY WED

♥

'He says we need to be married before - yeah, you guessed it - before he'll turn me into a vampire. He's such a traditionalist! My point to him is that traditionally a human marries another human, and that, technically, he's too dead to legally marry. So why are we waiting?'

As explained previously, vampires have a strange relationship with their own immortality. Most of them love it, but they wouldn't wish it on just anyone.

In addition, most vampires were brought up in an age where marriage was simply the done thing. If you wanted to live with someone, you got married. If you were having a child with someone, you got married (quickly). If you wanted to deprive someone of their life force until they were a walking shell with no soul, you guessed it, you got married.

Your wannabe-fiancé could have many reasons for his marriage bargain.

He could be insisting on marriage as a stalling technique, because he's not ready to commit to eternity with you. It's funny really; using the threat of commitment to avoid commitment.

Maybe he's not confident he can turn you safely. There's a huge risk of him losing you, even if he's done it before.

He could genuinely think it's the only right thing to do. Make an honest woman of you before he makes a devil of you.

Or maybe he just really wants to marry you. It doesn't take a genius to deduce that you're not that into weddings. He probably knows you'd take some convincing to say 'yes', then drag your feet over setting a date, and try to get away with just having a commitment ceremony, if he didn't dangle the carrot of immortality in front of your nose.

Whatever his reasons, it's clear you've got nothing to lose by just throwing caution to the wind and marrying him. Let him buy you a ring and wear it proudly. And try not to go around complaining about what a drag it is to be getting married, poor you, being loved by someone who wants to be yours forever, boo-hoo, and having to throw a massive party and wear a nice dress, or some single friend is going to punch you out.

TIP 84
VAMPIRE MOTHER-IN-LAW

♥

'Am I obliged to invite his female "relatives" to a hen's night?'

I'm afraid it's only polite to issue invitations to both sides of the family.

If you're worried about how well the 'cold ones' will mix with your incredibly human friends and relatives, don't. Let them worry about explaining their translucent skin, incredible beauty and reluctance to try the bar snacks. They're the ones walking around being vampires all over the place, they're not your responsibility.

So invite them and if they think they won't fit in, they'll stay away for your sake.

Oh, but if the very thought of mixing the two sides of the family is just too stressful for words, then save it for the wedding day (or rather night) and host an afternoon garden tea, so that your husband-to-be's rellies won't be able to go and also won't feel like they're missing out on anything fun.

BUCK'S NIGHT

♥

'I was really surprised to find out he's going to have a bachelor party. What happens at a vampire buck's night? If it's something to do with strippers, I don't want to know ...'

You don't want to know.

A DRINK TO YOUR HEALTH

♥

'How do we cater for the wedding guests who don't drink Champagne?'

First of all, you remove all talk of toasting from the proceedings. Nobody should 'raise a glass' to the bride and groom, because there is just no nice way for all guests to do it. Even the least murderous option involves squeezing a rat over a wine glass, and there's no way anyone's thinking about the health of the happy couple while this is going on in the room.

Stage the reception somewhere dimly lit and serve platters rather than a sit-down dinner. People at an informal party such as this don't notice who is drinking and who isn't. You'll know this from the times you stayed sober at someone's farewell drinks. People just assume you're drinking too, and tell you all sorts of amazing secrets.

The perfect vampire–human reception is a garden party, because fairy lights make even the mortal guests look eternally young and any immortals who get peckish can dart into the undergrowth for a quick tipple of the hard stuff.

WHERE'S THE GROOM?

♥

'I want to have a picture to hang to commemorate our big day. Is it true that no vampire can be seen in a photograph and, if so, how long do you think an oil painter would take to do a wedding party of twelve?'

I'm struggling to believe that you're at the nuptials stage and haven't even nailed down the basics. Now for some quick revision:

You *can't* see him in a mirror. You *can* see him in a photo.

You may be confused because vampires can only be photographed at night and on a long exposure. So, if they wished to, they could move fast enough to not appear on the film.

Photographing vampires is a bit trickier than photographing humans. Your beau and his relatives definitely cannot be photographed in daylight, no matter what charms they employ, as their skin will flare (yes, Twihards, you could say 'sparkle').

When taking your moonlit photos, you will need a quality film camera. A basic digital camera on a low-light filter will capture them as ghostly images, and don't even think about using the flash. If you have an in-phone camera you may as well just use it to call someone and describe what your vampire looks like, because it definitely won't work.

The good news is that means no-one can Twit-pic the ceremony and nobody will end up tagged on Facebook.

So it's best to get the photos done by a vampire who knows cameras. They'll have worked out all the tricks.

Or, by all means, get a portrait painted. It sounds like a classy idea. But you should bear in mind that even a very fast painter will take at least thirty-six hours to finish a quality oil portrait of a wedding party that size. Are you willing to delay the honeymoon? I wouldn't …

HONEYMOONLIGHT

💗

'What are the most romantic cities by night? I always imagined I'd spend my honeymoon lying on a tropical beach, but that doesn't seem so likely any more ...'

Some of those tropical beach-type honeymoon locations can actually have great nightlife, so perhaps you don't need to give up on that fantasy. You can enjoy some moonlight swimming, explore (and feed in) the tropical forests nearby and dance at the late-night beach bars. And then, while he's sleeping, you can sneak out for an hour and work on your much-neglected tan.

But there are some amazing cities that are alive all night that might offer more entertainment for a honeymooning couple.

Any big city you can reach by driving is worth considering. A car trip might seem unromantic, but you save all the hassles of flying with someone who's afraid of sunlight. Besides, when you're in love, anything's fun. Even a car trip. And he can drive really fast.

If you've got the cash to travel further, don't be afraid of a cliché; Paris is the perfect city to spend evenings in. The

Eiffel Tower lit up from below, the view of the sleeping city from the Sacré Cœur, the neon signs and trashy shows of the Moulin Rouge and the eerily quiet banks of the Seine at 4 am. Trust me, if you go there with your beloved, you'll talk like a tourism campaign too. It's just the most romantic city.

The only trouble is how to get there. I suggest the time-consuming and expensive method of short evening flights with stopovers in cities along the way. It's better than having to put your newlywed husband in the hold.

PRYING EYES

♥

'I can't be sure, but I think some people in town know what he is. So far, it's just the town crazies, and nobody really listens to them, but how do I know when too many people suspect the truth and we have to leave?'

Trust him, he'll know. He's had to move on many times before and he's an expert in hearing the suspicions in people's minds, well before they even realise they're having them.

You're probably right about the town crazies though. I'll bet they have noticed. That's the thing about crazy folks, their minds are freed up enough to see what other people can't. But for every viable idea they have, there'll be another one that's completely off the wall that they can't wait to tell you, like: 'When I was in the hospital, the doctors swapped my feet with the guy's in the next bed. That's why I don't walk so good, and also why I've got no money – his toes steal it all while I'm sleeping. Hey, do you have a knife I could use to cut them off?'

Who knows, maybe that's true too. Weirder things have happened. A vampire made you breakfast today. Who'd believe that?

TIP 90
BORN TO RUN

♥

'One thing I'm starting to understand about vampire life is that you can only live in one place for so long, and then you have to create new identities and move on. So when the time comes, do we flee together or separately?'

It's a smart question, because even though it feels easier to leave together, the sudden disappearance of a couple can end up looking more suspicious than if he just goes and leaves you to explain his absence for a few years before following on.

Yeah, I said a few years. I knew you wouldn't like that. But your man could come and visit you regularly, while he's setting up another life for both of you far away. Then you make your excuses – a new job or a change of scenery – and follow him.

This is a safer option because you have friends or family who may want to try and track you down and a couple is much easier to find, if they think you fled together.

In future moves, when you don't have so many ties, you will be able to just leave as a couple. But the first time, do it safely.

Keep in mind that for every identity change you make, you will need to open a new Facebook account, and all your old ones will need at least nominal maintenance to avoid people becoming concerned. For a while at least. Nobody really notices when somebody disappears off Facebook, if they don't announce their departure with a status update. Even if they do, people don't really notice.

Except maybe your mum. Which is another reason it's annoying that your mother discovered Facebook.

BIRDS OF A FEATHER

♥

'Is it better to go somewhere where there's other vampires?'

You have to be careful. While their presence indicates that the town is an ideal location for vampire life, they may react badly to the threat of new arrivals. Too many vampires means too many dead bodies (animal or human), which means everyone has to move on sooner.

You're better off finding a place where your man's hunting ground doesn't overlap with any other blood-suckers' territory. More than one set of vampires can live in an area, but they will want to establish contact and build a friendship before becoming housemates.

If a town seems really perfect, the process is similar to finding a table at a club. You hover nearby and as soon as it's free, you move in. Hopefully they haven't left too many spills that need mopping up.

WITNESS PROTECTION PROGRAM

💜

'What's the best story to tell people upon arriving in a new town?'

It's so much easier to invent appropriate lives for yourselves nowadays because of the host of valid jobs one can pretend to do from home, at odd hours of the day – jobs that didn't exist fifty years ago. Think about it. Your guy could be a web designer, electronic music producer, professional eBayer, or he could even be writing a book – lord knows that keeps you up all night.

As far as inventing a reason for choosing their town or city, never underestimate people's loyalty to the place they live. Tell them you came into a small inheritance and had always wanted to live here. It won't sound suspicious at all to them, because of course their town is the best place in the world.

TIP 93
HAPPY ENDING

♥

'That boy on the train? He came back. We ride the train together at night and get off at different stops and walk around the city for hours. We've still barely spoken, but I know that he is a good vampire and he would never hurt me and I'd give up everything to be with him. In fact, I think I'm going to. He says he's leaving soon and told me I should come. Is he telling the truth when he says he can look after me?'

Oh … sorry, God, one sec … I just came over a bit dizzy for a moment. Oh … I think I'm in love with him too. What's his name? I want to call it out in my dreams.

I say, follow him wherever he wants you to go. But take plenty of nice clothes, don't do anything illegal and call home every week so no-one worries about you. Plus, make sure you've always got enough money in the bank for a train ticket home.

I'm not gonna promise that it's all going to work out, because if I'm honest he sounds a bit flakey and not entirely able to even look after himself, let alone you. But whatever, what is life for, if not falling hard for the wrong people.

At the end of it, if you survive, you'll make a fortune turning it into a movie script.

ETERNITY FOR THE EASILY BORED

♥

'I'm considering immortality but I'm a workaholic who can't sit still. Will I be able to cope with having all that time on my hands?'

This is a reasonable concern to have. You are the sort of person who has a minor stroke if you have to wait ten minutes at a bus stop, and that's even with a BlackBerry full of emails to distract you. You spend the first ten days of an eleven-day holiday waking up at 6 am and making lists of people to write postcards to. You've done that, haven't you? Yeah, me too. Do you ever end up sending any of those postcards? No, me neither.

So how will you deal with the first ten hours, let alone ten decades, of immortality?

Trust me, you'll love it.

Through your new vampire eyes even the boring things of the world will seem endlessly fascinating. The best way to imagine it is like when the sun comes out from behind a cloud and everything suddenly becomes more 'real'. Except that you'll no longer be seeing the sunlight come out from behind a cloud, you'll be tucked up in your dark place when that happens. You will have to watch sunlight come out from behind clouds on TV. And you may even end up doing that, because like I said, even boring things will be endlessly fascinating.

You will, of course, retain some of your old workaholic personality, but you will find a new peace, courtesy of the knowledge that you do now, literally, have all the time in the world to get things done.

You will also revel in your new ability to get those things done faster and more efficiently, when you want to. But you won't want to, because becoming a vampire is simply going to chill you out. You'll learn to sit still and I guarantee you'll stop waking up at 6 am.

For your peace of mind, why not get into the zone ahead of time and practise seeing life as a vampire does? At one point in your life, you must have sat on a park bench and noticed how the breeze played on the leaves of the trees above your head? See if you can learn to do this for a few hours a day. That way, even if you don't end up choosing immortality, you'll probably live longer.

Don't be surprised if your world doesn't fall apart when you sit still for a while. At worst you might miss an episode of your favourite TV show, but don't worry, you'll have eternity to catch up when they release the box set.

WHAT HAPPENED TO HER?

♥

'When I change, people will be able to tell something's happened to me, won't they? Should I move away or fake my own death?'

There's something appropriate about faking your own death, because you will, for a few seconds during the process, be dead. Then afterwards you'll be, well, sort of ultra-dead. As horrible as it is to create a tragic scenario like that, it helps to drive home the seriousness of what you're about to do.

But it's cruel to those who love you. A much more generous act on your part would be to invent a disappearance that helps people let go of you, simply because you suddenly seem so, well, lame …

I'd suggest joining a crazy celebrity cult, except they have some crazy celebrity lawyers working for them, so I won't name any names. I will just say that if you tell your friends and family you've signed up with one of these movements, you can guarantee they won't expect to hear from you again, and nor will they want to. And no-one will be surprised when all the money disappears from your account.

TIP 96
LOVE THYSELF

♥

'I'm afraid. As much as I love him and want to be with him forever – and I do, more than anything – I can't bear the thought of putting up with myself forever.'

Oh, wow, lady, we've all felt like that before, but you shouldn't go into eternity thinking such depressing thoughts. In fact, you shouldn't feel like that for more than a day or two at a time, once a month, at most. Have you ever talked to someone about how little you like yourself?

There are professionals trained to help you work through these sorts of esteem problems. Maybe it'd be a good idea to have a month or two of weekly sessions, to feel better about yourself so that you can decide with a clear mind whether you're ready to die and be reborn as a blood-sucking creature of the night.

Don't tell your psych all of that, obviously. Just tell him the first bit about wanting to feel better about yourself, otherwise you'll be in for a lot more than just a month or two of sessions.

Before you take any steps towards becoming a vampire, you owe it to yourself to learn to like who you are. After all, you have to credit your one-and-only with *some* taste. He's decided he wants to put up with you forever, hasn't he? Why wouldn't you be able to?

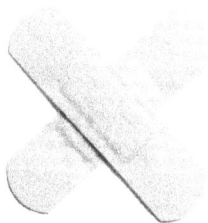

TIP 97

COMMITMENT-PHOBE

♥

'Can't I just go half-half?'

Um, what do you mean, exactly, when you say 'half-half'? No, sorry, I'm just really curious to see what you think that would entail. You think you'd still be able to go hang out with friends during the day but you'd just need lots of sunscreen? And you could, like, drink blood, but you could also still eat ice cream? And you wouldn't live forever, only half of forever? And how long would that be exactly?

The problem is that actually, halfway between being a human and being a vampire, is being dead.

If your inclination is to go half-half, whatever you think that might be, I think you're best off staying human, and just buying a set of fake fangs.

TIP 98
COOLING-OFF PERIOD

❤

'Ooops. I've gone immortal, but I've found out my old boyfriend wants to get back with me. I think I've made him jealous enough, how do I change back now?'

Ahhhh … what we have here is an example of not reading the fine print. Actually, I think it's pretty widely understood, even by people who don't know much about vampires, that immortality is a one-way street.

Well, not completely one-way. Here's what you do. You tell your other boyfriend, the one who's a vampire and who's gone through hell to change you over, that you've changed your mind, you only wanted to make the other guy jealous, and that you don't want to be a vampire anymore now, please.

Then all he has to do is put a stake through your heart, cut off your head and burn your remains. Then you'll be human again. Oh, sorry did I say human? I meant dead. But you won't be a vampire anymore, so job well done.

FOREVER EVER

♥

'I know I'm in it forever, but how can I be sure he is? I don't want to wind up a sad, single lady vampire, walking the Earth for eternity, heartbroken.'

Yeah, that's what we're all afraid of. The only thing worse than heartbreak is an eternity of heartbreak.

Admittedly the stakes are higher in this case, but it's really the same as when you're dealing with human men. You just have to take a guy's word for it. Just like he's taking your word for it – how can he be sure you're in it forever? Well, actually, he can read your mind, so he can be completely sure, but still … What I'm saying is you have to have trust.

It's funny to think that you're capable of trusting him to be strong enough not to kill you, but you're worried about trusting him to stay in love with you.

The great thing about love is that it's completely worth the risk. Love is worth getting tattoos for, losing jobs over and behaving like a dickhead for. And did you regret any of those things? No. A bit, maybe. But not much.

How much could you regret becoming a vampire?

Wait, don't answer that.

UGLY ETERNITY

❤

'Okay, so, today's the day we planned to do it. But I've woken up and I'm having the worst bad hair day. Will I have bad hair for eternity? Also, I have this huge pimple on my chin and I don't want that forever ...'

You've seen the magical good-lookingness of vampires. You've witnessed it close up. What do you think? You think it's possible to have bad hair as an immortal?

As a vampire, you will look exactly as you do now, but nothing like you do now.

You will still have to wash your hair, but not because it gets greasy, just because left long enough it will eventually get dust and leaves in it.

If you did have that pimple for eternity, it would be the most strangely attractive pimple the world had ever seen. People would fall to their knees and worship that pimple. But there's no need to worry, because the pimple is akin to a wound – it's a tiny, infected pore – and thus will disappear shortly after your skin's ability to regenerate kicks in.

So don't paint your nails and don't pluck your eyebrows, don't even bother with make-up today. Everything is perfect just where it is. Now let him work his magic.

TIP 101
THE END

♥

'So ... what's it like?'

When you find out, let me know.

THANKS

♥

First times are so much better with someone experienced holding your hand. I am therefore overflowing with gratitude for the delightful Karen Penning who brought me such an alluring idea and then plied me with the praise necessary to keep me focused! Thanks go to her friends at ABC Books/HarperCollins, in particular Gillian Hutchison and Chren Byng, who worked tirelessly to beat my words into publishable shape.

I would also like to express huge appreciation to all of my vampire-inclined friends, for their questions and feedback. I would never have managed to come up with 101 tips without their genuine, selfish interest in the topic. Two friends stand above the rest: Erin Zamagni for loaning me all her books, and Libby Klysz, who doesn't even like vampires, but does hope one day to marry 'good punctuation'.

Lastly I must thank my husband for offering his ongoing support in the form of frequent joke suggestions, infrequent cups of tea and real-life experience of tall, dark, handsome and sun-avoidant men.

www.ingramcontent.com/pod-product-compliance
Lightning Source LLC
Chambersburg PA
CBHW032138020426
42334CB00016B/1203